FROM KYOTO TO PARIS—TRANSITIONING THE CLEAN DEVELOPMENT MECHANISM

OCTOBER 2021

ADB

ASIAN DEVELOPMENT BANK

Contents

Tables, Figures, and Boxes

BOXES

Foreword

Climate change affects many aspects of day-to-day life as the world experiences a sharp increase in climate shocks and stresses. Floods, droughts, cyclones, and heat strains already impact livelihoods, food and water security, and the health of billions of people. In August 2021, the Intergovernmental Panel on Climate Change published its Sixth Assessment Report and reiterated the scale of the climate change challenge. Unlike the first five assessment reports, however, this report sounded an alarm and an urgent call for action: under all emission scenarios, the global surface temperature will continue to increase significantly until at least the middle of this century. There is a 50% chance in all scenarios that we will reach the 1.5°C target between 2021 and 2040. However, if the world takes very ambitious action to curb emissions in the 2020s, it is still possible to limit warming to 1.5°C by the end of the century.

Although the climate impacts that the world is already experiencing and the projections of what is to come are alarming, there is still a substantial gap in global efforts to meet the Paris Agreement goals. Policies in place today are projected to result in approximately 2.9°C of warming above pre-industrial levels, which far exceeds those internationally agreed goals. While the recent wave of net-zero-emissions pledges from many countries is promising, it is critical that we ensure that all countries increase their mitigation ambition, and that pledges and emission reduction targets are translated into long-term strategies and immediate action.

Strategy 2030 of the Asian Development Bank (ADB) reflects its vision to achieve a prosperous, inclusive, resilient, and sustainable Asia and the Pacific, while sustaining efforts to eradicate extreme poverty. Tackling climate change, building climate and disaster resilience, and enhancing environmental sustainability is one of the operational strategies of ADB's Strategy 2030. In 2018, ADB committed to ensuring at least 75% of the total number of its operations support climate action and its own climate finance resources reach at least a cumulative $80 billion by 2030. The bank has announced it is increasing climate financing for developing member countries (DMCs) to $100 billion in 2019–2030. Doing so would contribute to transforming the energy sector in DMCs. However, additional resources will be required, and a variety of policy instruments are needed to mobilize additional finance.

Carbon pricing is a key component of the broader architecture of climate policy instruments that can enable countries to raise mitigation ambition and achieve emission reductions that are sufficient to meet the Paris Agreement Goals. Clear and predictable carbon price signals in domestic and international markets can both enhance the economic competitiveness of low-carbon technologies and help countries achieve the climate targets that are articulated in their respective Nationally Determined Contributions cost-effectively. International carbon markets as envisaged under Article 6 of the Paris Agreement are promising instruments for mobilizing carbon finance and disseminating advanced low-carbon technologies, both of which are critical to enabling a transition toward net-zero emissions.

The Asia and Pacific region embodies a wealth of experience and expertise in operationalizing international carbon markets to mobilize carbon finance and support greenhouse gas mitigation activities. Approximately 80% of all registered Subsidiary Body for Scientific and Technological Advice (CDM) activities are hosted in the region. This gives Parties in the region a particular stake in the outcomes of the negotiations regarding the transitioning of aspects of the CDM into the Paris framework, as well as an interest in better understanding what the outcomes of the negotiations on this issue may be and how different Parties may be affected.

Experience from previous engagement with the CDM will come into play as Parties endeavor to develop strategies for utilizing carbon markets to incentivize new mitigation actions. For countries that host existing portfolios of registered CDM activities (projects and Program of Activities), two aspects of such strategic planning are the extent to which such activities and the carbon credits that they generated pre-2020 can and will transition for use under the Paris Agreement. International eligibility requirements for such transitions are two of three aspects of the CDM transition that will be negotiated at the 26th Conference of the Parties (COP26). The third involves the transition of methodologies and relevant components of the international institutional infrastructure.

The guidance and rules for operationalizing international carbon markets under Article 6 have yet to be finalized. Key decisions in this regard are expected to be made at the COP26 to the United Nations Framework Convention on Climate Change (UNFCCC) in November 2021. Eligibility rules and guidelines for each of the three components of the CDM transition will be on the table. Stakeholders are anxiously awaiting the outcome of these negotiations.

In light of the upcoming negotiations at COP26, ADB hopes that this publication will shed light on complex political and technical issues surrounding the CDM transition to policy makers, Article 6 negotiators, and the owners of CDM activities. It is my sincere hope to see a successful outcome at COP26 and for countries to shift gears toward operationalizing international carbon markets as envisaged under Article 6 of the Paris Agreement.

Bruno Carrasco
Director General, concurrently Chief Compliance Officer
Sustainable Development and Climate Change Department
Asian Development Bank

Preface

In 2015, the Parties to the United Nations Framework Convention on Climate Change adopted the Paris Agreement, which sets targets for limiting climate change that necessitate ambitious efforts of all Parties to reduce their greenhouse gas emissions. The Paris Agreement has inspired renewed interest in market-based mechanisms for stimulating mitigation action and reflects the desire of Parties to be free to choose among different approaches to achieving national emissions targets. Through its ongoing Carbon Market Program, ADB supports its DMCs on the development and use of market-based mechanisms and will continue to play a leadership role in the development of carbon markets under Article 6 of the Paris Agreement. As part of these efforts, ADB strives to contribute to knowledge and capacity building to encourage deeper understanding of the ongoing international discussions and technical options available for the development and implementation of market-based approaches under Article 6.

The bottom–up architecture of the Article 6 instruments that enable the use of carbon markets brings complexity to international market-based cooperation. This complexity is reflected in the international negotiations on guidance, rules, modalities, and procedures for operationalizing Articles 6.2 and 6.4; and the difficulties that have been faced in finalizing these issues in what is commonly referred to as the Article 6 Rulebook. The coronavirus disease 2019 (COVID-19) pandemic has contributed to delaying the adoption of the Rulebook, but the next negotiation round will take place at COP26, in November 2021, in Glasgow.

As the international climate community advances toward finalizing the Article 6 Rulebook, policy makers, negotiators, and the owners of CDM activities in the Asia and Pacific region need to understand the CDM transition issues being negotiated. This is important, not only to enable DMC stakeholders to contribute to the finalization of the Article 6 Rulebook, but also to facilitate host country and private sector planning and preparations for participating in operationalizing carbon markets under Article 6. This publication provides a mapping of both political and technical aspects of the key issues, implications of the solutions that are being discussed, and considerations and challenges for those countries in the region that are hosts to registered CDM activities.

The CDM transition comprises three elements: (i) methodologies and relevant components of the international institutional infrastructure, (ii) mitigation activities, and (iii) credits. Adopting CDM methodologies and infrastructure is relatively uncontroversial. All three aspects have been discussed under previous Article 6 negotiations, and the negotiations at COP25 in Madrid and discussions at the Subsidiary Body for Scientific and Technological Advice (SBSTA) 46 in June 2017 have provided some clarity regarding Parties' positions and the directions in which an agreement may go.

These negotiations and discussions indicate that the transition of methodologies and parts of the CDM infrastructure are relatively uncontroversial. The resources accrued through investment in the CDM in both the public and private sectors—including experience, knowledge, and institutional capacity—are broadly acknowledged as valuable and applicable to international carbon markets under the Paris Agreement, and the experience and expertise acquired— with respect to governance, methodological approaches and project administration, and operation—are still relevant. It is also anticipated that small-scale CDM activities may receive expedited status for transition, which would benefit least developed countries and small island developing states (SIDS). There is also broad support for the transitioning of some (but not all) CDM activities. This support is grounded in an understanding that many current CDM activities are dependent on carbon market revenue to continue to operate. It may be possible to agree to registration cutoff dates as eligibility criteria for the transition of both CDM activities and credits. However, the third and final iteration of the Madrid text indicates that the criteria for transitioning CDM activities may not include a cutoff date but, rather, only a deadline for completing the transition process (which includes CDM de-registration and re-registration under the new Article 6.4 mechanism or a 6.2 mechanism). However, the transition and use of CDM credits issued before 2020 for Nationally Determined Contribution (NDC) compliance purposes under the Paris Agreement is a contentious political issue. There is concern that transitioning pre-2020 CDM credits could undermine efforts to stimulate new mitigation action. Informal negotiations under SBSTA 46 revealed that Parties maintain diverging positions regarding the transition of carbon credits, across the full spectrum from opposing that any credits to transition, to applying various types of filtering criteria, to allowing a full transition of all issued credits.

Any aspect of the CDM that transitions for use under Article 6 will need to be adapted. This is true for emerging mechanisms under both Article 6.2 and 6.4, but particularly important with respect to the transitioning of methodologies, infrastructure, and activities to the new mechanism under Article 6.4; and this adaptation work cannot occur until after the overarching Rulebook issues have been resolved. Agreement on those issues will greatly reduce uncertainty and enable planning on the part of host country governments and the owners of CDM activities alike.

It is our hope that this publication will be useful in increasing knowledge and understanding of the negotiations regarding the CDM transition and their implications for the Asia and Pacific region. Armed with this knowledge and understanding, ADB hopes that stakeholders in the region will be better prepared to engage in discussions with the aim of contributing to finalizing the Article 6 Rulebook and advancing toward operationalizing Article 6 of the Paris Agreement.

Virender Kumar Duggal
Principal Climate Change Specialist
Sustainable Development and Climate Change Department
Asian Development Bank

Acknowledgments

From Kyoto to Paris—Transitioning the Clean Development Mechanism has been developed by the Asian Development Bank (ADB) in its implementation of the regional capacity development technical assistance project under Article 6 Support Facility (A6SF) of the Carbon Market Program within its Sustainable Development and Climate Change Department (SDCC).

Virender Kumar Duggal, principal climate change specialist, Climate Change and Disaster Risk Management Division, ADB, conceptualized and guided development of this knowledge product.

The knowledge product has been developed with inputs from a team of experts engaged under ADB's ongoing Technical Assistance 9695: Establishing a Support Facility for Article 6 of the Paris Agreement, which included Rastraraj Bhandari, Deborah Cornland, Axel Michaelowa, Johan Nylander, and Richa Verma—all of whom are greatly appreciated. This knowledge product has also benefited from technical inputs from other members of ADB's Carbon Market Program—which is deeply appreciated—most notably from Takeshi Miyata, climate change specialist; and Brij Mohan, CDM technical specialist. Thomas Forth, senior advisor, Federal Ministry for the Environment, Nature Conservation, Building and Nuclear Safety, Germany; and Nils Westling and Ida Hamilton, program managers at the Swedish Energy Agency, also provided their valuable inputs, which is sincerely appreciated.

This knowledge product has hugely benefited from the peer review conducted by the Institute for Global Environmental Strategies, Japan, which is sincerely acknowledged and appreciated.

The timely publication of this report was made possible by the valuable coordination and administrative support of Janet Arlene R. Amponin, Anna Liza Cinco, Ken Edward Concepcion, Ketchie Molina, Ghia V. Rabanal, and Ellen May Reynes. Monina Gamboa edited the report. Joseph Manglicmot did the layout and composition. Francis Manio created the cover design. Levi Lusterio proofread the report and Jess Macasaet handled the page proof check. Their diligent inputs are greatly acknowledged and appreciated.

Abbreviations

A6.4ER	Article 6, paragraph 4, emission reduction
AAU	assigned amount unit
ADB	Asian Development Bank
AEPC	Alternative Energy Promotion Center
AOSIS	Alliance of Small Island States
CDM	Clean Development Mechanism
CER	certified emission reduction
CMA	Conference of the Parties serving as the meeting of the Parties to the Paris Agreement
CMP	Conference of the Parties serving as the meeting of the Parties to the Kyoto Protocol
COP	Conference of the Parties to the UNFCCC
CORSIA	Carbon Offsetting and Reduction Scheme for International Aviation
CPA	component project activity
DMC	developing member country
DNA	designated national authority
DOE	designated operational entity
EB	Executive Board (CDM)
EIG	Environmental Integrity Group
ERU	emission reduction unit
ETS	Emissions Trading Scheme
EU	European Union
FVA	Framework for Various Approaches
GHG	greenhouse gas
IET	International Emission Trading
ITMO	internationally transferred mitigation outcome
JCM	joint crediting mechanism
JISC	Joint Implementation Supervisory Committee
KP	Kyoto Protocol
Lao PDR	Lao Peoples Democratic Republic
LDC	least developed country
MPGs	modalities, procedures, and guidelines
MRV	monitoring, reporting, and verification
NDC	Nationally Determined Contribution
NMM	New Market-based Mechanism
OMGE	Overall Mitigation in Global Emissions
POA	program of activities
PRC	People's Republic of China
RMP	rules, modalities, and procedures
SBSTA	Subsidiary Body for Scientific and Technological Advice

SIDS   small island developing state
UNEP DTU   United Nations Environment Programme and the Technical University of Denmark
UNFCCC   United Nations Framework Convention on Climate Change

Executive Summary

Discussions and negotiations regarding the transition from the Clean Development Mechanism (CDM) to Article 6 under the Paris Agreement typically address the transition of three different parts of the CDM: (i) baseline and monitoring methodologies and relevant components of the international institutional infrastructure, (ii) activities (i.e., CDM projects and Programs of Activities [POAs]), and (iii) emissions credits or Certified Emission Reductions (CERs). This study focuses on the transition of CDM activities to the Article 6.4 mechanism and the transition of CERs for compliance with mitigation commitments expressed in Nationally Determined Contributions (NDCs).

Transitioning the relevant CDM infrastructure to Article 6 is not controversial as it is mainly a question of agreeing on a process at the international level. Transition of methodologies is somewhat contested, but there are indications that CDM methodologies may be transitioned if complemented by tools that enable consistency with Article 6 principles. Similarly, there seems to be general agreement that at least some activities that meet Article 6.4 eligibility criteria and are re-authorized by their host countries should be allowed to transition into the Paris Agreement under Article 6.4. However, two issues that have yet to be resolved are what those eligibility criteria will be (which will be determined by the Parties through negotiation) and how transitions will be implemented, i.e., the transition rules and associated transition costs, which also will involve priorities and criteria determined by host countries. The draft negotiation texts from the 25th Conference of the Parties (COP25) in Madrid provide some indication to the possible criteria that may be used with regard to activity transition and the potential exemptions that could be made. However, important gaps remain, pushing key aspects of operationalization to future decisions by the Subsidiary Body for Scientific and Technical Advice (SBSTA), the Supervisory Body of the Article 6.4. mechanism, and possibly both the Conference of the Parties serving as the meeting of the Parties to the Kyoto Protocol (CMP) and Conference of the Parties serving as the meeting of the Parties to the Paris Agreement (CMA)—the Conferences of the Parties being Members of the Kyoto Protocol and the Paris Agreement.

On the other hand, the transition of CERs i.e., whether and to what extent Kyoto Protocol units can be used in the Paris Agreement period for NDC compliance, is highly controversial. While proponents of CER transition focus on the need to provide investor confidence and to ensure the significant investments in CDM continue to generate revenues, others argue that CER transition can negatively impact the market price of carbon credits and undermine environmental integrity and the overall ambition of the Paris Agreement. The issue of CER transition is now also discussed in the context of Article 6.2 because some countries want to prevent that governments transition CERs bilaterally under Article 6.2 or use CERs generated in their jurisdiction toward their own NDC in case of prohibition of CER transition to Article 6.4.

Based on options listed in the Madrid texts, proposals by Parties to the Paris Agreement and discussions in the academic and grey literature, the report analyzes how different criteria or filters would affect the transition of both CDM activities and CERs.

Transition of Clean Development Mechanism Activities

Applying a cutoff date as a criterion for the transition of activities would have a strong impact on the volume of activities that can be transitioned. Currently, in the developing member countries (DMCs) of the Asian Development Bank (ADB), only 33% of the registered projects remain active (34% of all small-scale and 31% of all large-scale projects). If a registration cutoff of 1 January 2013 were adopted, only 18% (389) of all active CDM projects and 29% (44) of all active POAs would be eligible for transition. This share would be reduced to 4.6% (98) for all active CDM projects and 12% (18) of all active POAs if a registration date cutoff of 1 January 2016 were applied. This cutoff date would limit the eligible activity transition volumes to zero or near zero for the DMC host countries with large portfolios (the People's Republic of China, Malaysia, Thailand, and Viet Nam). A late cutoff date seems to favor least developed countries (LDCs) in Asia and the Pacific.

The proposal to apply a deadline for completing the transition (CDM de-registration and re-registration under Article 6.4) instead of a cutoff date would be contingent on the ability to quickly set up the Article 6.4 infrastructure and could, in any way, lead to a stampede of activity developers like the one witnessed under the CDM in 2012 that could overwhelm regulators. Creation of a fast track for small- and micro-scale activities and POAs, which is not contested, would benefit the LDCs.

Experience from CDM negotiations would imply that Parties are not likely to agree to excluding specific types of activities from transitioning to Article 6 mechanisms, even if pressure has increased to do so. However, it might be possible that some criteria may be decided in future decisions, either by the CMA or by the Supervisory Body of the Article 6.4 mechanism.

Transition of Certified Emission Reductions

From the viewpoint of activity developers, transition of CERs is only relevant for the CERs that have been issued, but not yet sold; and for CERs that have not yet been issued, but that could be issued for vintages before 2021.[*] Many activity developers have stopped issuance in the years of low CER prices but have continued monitoring and thus would be able to request issuance for pre-2021 vintages.

In the Asia and Pacific region, 42% of issued CERs, i.e., a total of over 700 million, have not yet been used, compared to a global average of 55%. This relatively good performance is dominated by the PRC and India that have been able to sell about 60% of the issued CERs; for 14 out of 25 countries from the region, over 70% of CERs remain unused; for POAs, almost 90% of CERs remain unused. Looking at activity types, industrial gas projects, and solar and tidal energy have been able to sell a large share of their CERs, whereas energy efficiency, hybrid renewables, transport, and fugitive emissions-related activities have over 80% of unsold CERs. An analysis was performed based on three dates: 1 January 2008, 1 January 2013, and 1 January 2016, like the analysis for CDM activities. In total, about 430 million unused CERs can transition under a 2008 registration cutoff date from Asia and the Pacific. However, this volume falls to 75 million for the 2013 cutoff and just 4 million for the 2016 cutoff. For later cutoff dates, activity types shift from hydro and wind to energy efficiency and solar.

---

[*] UNFCCC. 2019. Matters relating to Article 6 of the Paris Agreement: Rules, modalities, and procedures for the mechanism established by Article 6, para. 4, of the Paris Agreement. *Proposal by the President.* Bonn. https://unfccc.int/documents/204686.

Regarding not yet issued, "dormant" CERs, an objective assessment is very difficult; estimates in the literature diverge widely depending on key assumptions regarding the continued operation of activities, continued monitoring, and the degree to which crediting periods have been renewed. It is clear that issuances have not been requested for a large share of emissions reductions achieved between 2013 and 2020, but no robust estimates can be made. Published estimates vary between 2 and 4 billion of "dormant" CERs.

Implications for Host Countries

The agreements made in the negotiations regarding the transition of CDM activities and CERs can influence their potential to participate in international carbon markets under Article 6. These considerations should inform their participation in the negotiations.

For countries hosting registered and still active CDM activities, it is important to consider how re-registration of CDM activities to Article 6 mechanisms may impact the achievement of their NDC targets. This strongly depends on whether corresponding adjustments need to be made for CER transactions leading to internationally transferred mitigation outcome (ITMO) transfers, which seems likely at the current status of negotiations. It becomes especially challenging if CERs for pre-2021 vintages can be transitioned, as these reflect mitigation that has happened outside of the NDC period. Here, the government needs to have a clear view of how to ensure that NDC achievement is not jeopardized by the CER transaction, which could, for example, be the case if the CDM activity no longer continues to generate greenhouse gas mitigation after the end of its crediting period. These issues must be considered regardless of whether a case-by-case, group, or blanket assessment approach to authorizing transitions is applied. It would also be useful to assess the process of CDM transition in terms of the capacities of their institutions that will shoulder operational responsibilities. The host country needs to make important decisions and implement procedures for authorizing the re-registration of activities. To do so, the host country can consider what approach it will adopt to assessing and authorizing activities for registration under Article 6.4 and utilizing that also for activities transitioning from the CDM.

CDM host countries would also gain from estimating what they can expect in terms of transition volumes. How many CDM activities are likely to request transition? If many activities are expected to transition, this would require an administrative effort from the host country. However, this would also depend on what options are available to activity owners. Some CDM activities may also be de-registered from the CDM and transition to the voluntary or domestic carbon crediting markets. Furthermore, how many CERs would be issued for pre-2021 vintages would depend on the expected CER price. If there are cutoff dates for re-registration, pressure on governments to process authorizations could become acute prior to the cutoff date.

Finally, irrespective of the outcomes on the transition of CDM activities and CERs in COP26 in Glasgow, host countries with experience in the CDM need to ensure that the human resources including experience, knowledge, as well as institutional capacity created under the CDM can be preserved and used for Article 6 purposes. These experiences and expertise, not only in the governance level, but also in the methodological as well as project levels, are crucial for countries' participation in the international carbon markets under Article 6 of the Paris Agreement.

1. Background

Objective

International carbon markets under the Kyoto Protocol, particularly the Clean Development Mechanism (CDM), have played a key role for greenhouse gas mitigation in Asian Development Bank (ADB) members. With the negotiations of the rulebook for international carbon markets under Article 6 of the Paris Agreement entering a critical phase at the 26th Conference of the Parties (COP26) in Glasgow in November 2021, the question of how CDM activities and/or methodologies and/or other infrastructure as well as Certified Emission Reductions (CERs) can be made available for use under the mechanism specified under Article 6.4. This "CDM transition" is of high relevance for developing countries which have been hosting CDM activities. More broadly, operationalizing a CDM transition will require decisions on a wide range of issues at both the international and national levels, including the adaptation of CDM methodologies to be consistent with the modalities of Article 6, eligibility requirements defining which CDM activities and CERs can be transitioned, decisions required by host countries, and the development of procedures for re-registering de-registered CDM activities.[1]

The aim of this study is to further the understanding of policy makers, Article 6 negotiators, and the owners of CDM activities (i.e., projects and Programs of Activities [POAs]) in ADB's developing member countries (DMCs) of key issues being negotiated regarding the CDM transition and their relevance to the Asia and Pacific region. It analyzes the CDM portfolios of ADB's DMCs and the regional implications of the CDM transition options being negotiated for transitioning existing CDM activities (projects and POAs) to Article 6.4 and CERs for use in complying with Nationally Determined Contributions (NDCs) under the Paris Agreement. A case study of Nepal is used to illustrate these issues through concrete examples.

The publication discusses criteria that may regulate the volume or type of CDM activities and CERs that may be allowed to transition. It should be noted that ADB does not have a position on how many or which types of CDM activities and CERs should be eligible for transition, nor does it have views or preferences regarding possible transition scenarios or regarding criteria for transition eligibility to be decided jointly by the Parties.

---

[1]   The CDM Executive Board (CDM EB) agreed to establish a procedure for de-registering projects and programs as part of a review of its standards procedures in 2015. De-registration requires written agreement of all project participants of the activity and a written no-objection of the Designated National Authorities (DNAs) of all Parties involved in the activity. As of October 2020, 12 projects had been de-registered.

The Clean Development Mechanism

The CDM is one of three flexible mechanisms established in 1997 under the Kyoto Protocol.[2] It came into operation through a prompt start in 2001 under detailed rules defined in the Marrakech Accords, allowing a pipeline of activities to be created in advance of the first commitment period of the Kyoto Protocol between 2008 and 2012. The Kyoto Protocol entered into force on 16 February 2005, enabling the detailed CDM rules to be formalized. The rules were adopted at the Conference of the Parties serving as the meeting of the Parties to the Kyoto Protocol (CMP1)/COP11 in Montreal later that year.

The CDM was created to enable activities that result in emission reductions in developing countries to generate emission credits (CERs) to be sold to industrialized countries for partially meeting emission reduction targets under the Kyoto Protocol. The CDM was designed with the aim to help host countries achieve sustainable development and reduce emissions, while giving industrialized countries some flexibility in how they meet their emission targets.[3] By 2021, the CDM had resulted in around 7,848 registered projects as well as around 355 Programs of Activities (POAs) and had issued over 2 billion CERs.[4]

ADB's DMCs have a considerable breadth of experience with the CDM: 82% of all registered CDM activities are hosted in the region.[5] However, the experience is not evenly distributed among ADB's DMCs. Some DMCs are host to several thousand CDM activities while others have hosted none or very few. In a previous ADB report, the involvement of DMCs in the CDM was grouped as shown in Table 1, which looks at countries that have specifically mentioned carbon markets in their NDCs.[6]

Table 1: Experience with Project-Based Mechanisms among Developing Member Countries Expressly Interested in Carbon Markets

Experience with Project-Based Mechanisms	Clean Development Mechanism only	Clean Development Mechanism and Joint Crediting Mechanism
Limited (<10 activities)	Armenia, Bhutan, Fiji, Nepal	Bangladesh, Mongolia
Moderate (10–100 activities)	Pakistan	Cambodia, Lao People's Democratic Republic
Advanced (>100 activities)	India, People's Republic of China	Indonesia, Thailand, Viet Nam

Source: B. Amarjargal et al. 2020. *Achieving Nationally Determined Contributions through Market Mechanisms in Asia and the Pacific*. Manila: ADB

Table 1 illustrates the variation in levels of involvement among DMCs that have hosted CDM activities. Two countries have the most experience as hosts to CDM activities: the People's Republic of China accounts for 58.4% of all activities registered in ADB's DMCs and India hosts 25.7%. Viet Nam (4%) and Indonesia (2.3%) have also hosted many CDM activities, and Malaysia and Thailand have each hosted 2.2%. ADB's DMCs also host over 150 POAs containing about 700 component project activities (CPAs). Many DMCs have none.

---

[2]   The Kyoto Protocol established Joint Implementation (Article 6), the Clean Development Mechanism (Article 12), and International Emissions Trading (Article 17). International emissions trading (IET) allows trade of emissions allowances ("Assigned Amount Units") between countries with quantitative targets (caps) under the Kyoto Protocol; it is not discussed further here.

[3]   UNFCCC. 2001. The Marrakesh Accords and The Marrakesh Declaration. https://unfccc.int/cop7/documents/accords_draft.pdf.

[4]   United Nations Environment Programme and the Technical University of Denmark (UNEP DTU). 2021. CDM pipeline, and POA pipeline. Copenhagen. www.cdmpipeline.org (accessed 19 September 2021).

[5]   In addition, the region hosts roughly 90% of all projects under the Joint Crediting Mechanism (JCM), a bilateral crediting mechanism developed by Japan, see Institute for Global Environmental Strategies (IGES). Joint Crediting Mechanism Database, 2019.

[6]   B. Amarjargal et al. 2020. *Achieving Nationally Determined Contributions through Market Mechanisms in Asia and the Pacific*. Manila: ADB

Box 1: The Clean Development Mechanism in a Nutshell

The basic principle underlying the Clean Development Mechanism (CDM) is a baseline-and-crediting approach. A baseline (i.e., "business-as-usual") emissions level is compared with the emissions level after the implementation of a mitigation activity, and the difference gives rise to emissions credits. A necessary condition is the existence of baseline and monitoring methodologies that are differentiated according to activity types. Methodologies can be submitted by anyone and, once approved by the mechanism regulator (the CDM Executive Board [CDM EB]), can be used by anyone.

The CDM EB must formally register activities before they can generate Certified Emission Reductions (CERs). Preconditions for registration are approval by the host country and a "validation" of consistency of the activity with the CDM rules by an accredited auditor or Designated Operational Entity (DOE). As emissions reductions must be real, measurable, and verifiable as well as "additional," here, it is checked that the activity is "additional," i.e., different from business as usual and not commercially attractive without the revenue from CER sales.

CERs are issued ex post by the CDM Executive Board after emissions reductions have been independently verified by DOEs.

Source: UNFCCC. *The Clean Development Mechanism.* https://unfccc.int/process-and-meetings/the-kyoto-protocol/mechanisms-under-the-kyoto-protocol/the-clean-development-mechanism.

Reforming or Replacing the Clean Development Mechanism Under the Paris Agreement

Given that there already is a baseline-and-crediting mechanism operating under the auspices of the United Nations Framework Convention on Climate Change (UNFCCC)—the CDM—why cannot it continue to operate and be used under the Paris Agreement? Can it simply be adjusted to the new climate regime? The technical answer is that the CDM belongs formally to the Kyoto Protocol and has no formal space or supporting provisions in the Paris Agreement framework. While the decision to adopt the Paris Agreement states that the new mechanisms should build on the experiences of the Kyoto Mechanisms,[7] it does not speak of the CDM specifically.

A more elaborate answer is that the development of the Paris Agreement and the international carbon market to be used thereunder is a result of a decade of negotiations, involving proposals for new UNFCCC market mechanisms and the development of market mechanisms outside the UNFCCC. Although the CDM was a success in terms of the quantities of registered activities and emission reductions it achieved, the mechanism has generated criticism since its inception, which has triggered both reform attempts and proposals for mechanisms designed differently.[8] The provisions in Article 6.4 include elements that some of the Parties have wanted to see in a new mechanism, for instance, a clear reference to an overall mitigation in global emissions.

---

[7]   UNFCCC. 2015. Adoption of the Paris Agreement. *Decision 1/CP.21.* Bonn. https://unfccc.int/resource/docs/2015/cop21/eng/10a01.pdf.
[8]   A. Michaelowa, I. Shishlov, and D. Brescia. 2019. *Evolution of international carbon markets: lessons for the Paris Agreement.* WIREs Climate Change. https://wires.onlinelibrary.wiley.com/doi/10.1002/wcc.613.

2. Article 6 of the Paris Agreement

The Paris Agreement differs significantly from the Kyoto Protocol in ways that have important implications for the design of the framework for market-based mechanisms. The Paris Agreement has a less centralized compliance regime than Kyoto that is built primarily on transparent reporting as the means for assessing progress against its objectives. Another key difference is that under the Kyoto Protocol, developing countries participated in the international carbon market as hosts for CDM activities without having mitigation targets on their own. Under the Paris Agreement, developing countries also have mitigation targets through their NDCs, and can participate in international carbon markets as sellers or buyers of internationally transferred mitigation outcomes (ITMOs).

Article 6 contains two carbon market routes.[9] Article 6.2 involves limited international oversight and covers cooperative approaches that lead to a transfer of ITMOs. Article 6.2 provides an accounting framework for managing all types of cooperative approaches, be it emissions trading between states, linking of Emissions Trading Schemes (ETSs), bilaterally or multilaterally designed, or agreed baseline-and-crediting mechanisms. In principle, countries are free to "relabel" CDM activities into activities under Article 6.2. For ITMO transactions under Article 6.2, countries are likely to have to apply "double bookkeeping" as was the case for industrialized countries under Joint Implementation, called "corresponding adjustments" in the Paris Agreement.

Article 6.4 creates a new mitigation and sustainable development mechanism with a governance structure subject to centralized oversight (as was the case under the CDM). It generates Article 6.4 emission reductions (A6.4ERs) that will then become ITMOs once internationally transferred.[10] Article 6.4 may take up CDM modalities and adopt elements of the CDM if Parties and international regulators are willing to do so. To what extent developing countries have to apply "corresponding adjustments" under the Article 6.4 mechanism is still heavily contested by a few countries.

---

[9] Article 6.8 which defines a nonmarket approach, is not discussed in this publication.
[10] The incorporation of Article 6.4 emission reductions to Article 6.2 accounting is still a matter of dispute in the UNFCCC negotiations.

3. What and How Much to Transition

Discussions and negotiations on the CDM transition typically focus on three different parts of the CDM: (i) methodologies and relevant components of the international institutional infrastructure, (ii) activities, and (iii) emission credits (CERs).[11] This study is focused on the transition of CDM activities to the Article 6.4 mechanism and the transition of CERs for compliance with mitigation commitments in NDCs, but it also touches upon the use of existing CDM methodologies and the accreditation system.

Given the long-term nature of the climate change challenge, ensuring regulatory continuity and the credibility of the UNFCCC process is important. Well-established international policy instruments should not be discarded lightheartedly.[12] Adapting relevant components of the existing international institutional structure of CDM for the new mechanism under Article 6.4 would save time and resources and could accelerate the start of the new mechanism.

Transitioning methodologies and components of international infrastructure is also resource-efficient. The infrastructure of the CDM was built over many years and constitutes a significant value. There are currently 252 approved CDM methodologies covering a wide range of activity types. The cost of developing a new methodology is at least $35,000[13] and more complex methodologies can cost up to $200,000.[14] Using these estimates, the implicit value of the CDM library of methodologies ranges from approximately $10 million to $50 million. However, transitioning CDM methodologies without adjusting them to take into account the requirement of contributing to an increase in ambition may lead to long-term detrimental effects on global mitigation.[15] Methodologies need to reflect emission reduction trajectories aligned with the Paris Agreement and countries' NDCs and should not apply concepts that inflate estimates of baseline emissions, such as suppressed demand.[16] It may be a challenge to get sufficient methodological expertise into the Article 6.4 support structure to enable rapid development of innovative methodologies (footnote 15).

[11]   L. Re and M. Vaidyula. 2019. Markets Negotiations under the Paris Agreement a technical analysis of two unresolved issues. *Climate Change Expert Group Paper* No. 2019(3). Paris: International Energy Agency (IEA) and Organisation for Economic Co-operation and Development (OECD). https://www.oecd.org/env/cc/Markets-negotiations-under-the-Paris-Agreement-a-technical-analysis-of-two-unresolved-issues.pdf.

[12]   A. Marcu and V. Duggal. 2019. *Negotiations on Article 6 of the Paris Agreement–Road to Madrid.* Manila: ADB.

[13]   United Nations Development Programme (UNDP). 2006. *The Clean Development Mechanism – An Assessment of Progress.* New York. https://www.uncclearn.org/sites/default/files/inventory/undp34.pdf.

[14]   S. Hoch et al. 2020. *Closing the Deal on "CDM Transition" – How COP 25 Defined New Guardrails for Compromise and What They Mean for Africa.* Freiburg: Climate Finance Innovators. https://www.climatefinanceinnovators.com/publication/closing-the-deal-on-cdm-transition/.

[15]   A. Michaelowa et al. 2020. *CDM method transformation: updating and transforming CDM methods for use in an Article 6 context.* Freiburg: Perspectives Climate Group GmbH. https://ercst.org/document/cdm-method-transformation-updating-and-transforming-cdm-methods-for-use-in-an-article-6-context/.

[16]   A. Michaelowa, H. Ahonen, and A. Espelage. 2021. Setting crediting baselines under Article 6 of the Paris Agreement. *CMM Working Group Discussion Paper.* Freiburg: Perspectives Climate Group GmbH https://www.perspectives.cc/public/fileadmin/user_upload/CMM-WG_Art_6_baselines_Final_layouted_v2__002_.pdf.

The CDM also established, for example, a system for accrediting independent entities to perform validation, verification, and certification. Globally, there are several dozen designated operational entities (DOEs) with significant capacity for validating and verifying mitigation actions and emission reductions. Adapting and transitioning components of the CDM infrastructure to Article 6.4 would save time, effort, and financial resources.

Transitioning CDM activities would help to regain the trust of private sector entities in the long-term stability of international carbon markets, making them more likely to participate in the mechanisms emerging under Article 6. Given that CDM activities can have crediting periods of up to 21 years (for projects) to 28 years (for POAs), or up to 60 years for forestry activities, many developers of CDM activities felt betrayed when demand for and the price of CERs collapsed in 2012 and the market did not recover. If the CDM is stopped from 2021 onward, a large share of CDM activities will be unable to complete their crediting periods. It is unlikely that private companies will engage in the Article 6 carbon markets if they perceive a significant risk of the markets for credits being unstable or cut short. Overall, allowing the transition of CDM activities would be a trust-enhancing measure that sends a signal to the private sector that the new market-based mechanisms will not just be "switched off."[17]

It has been argued that the existing pipeline of CDM activities may be ideally placed for scaling up mitigation action quickly and effectively under the new Article 6.4 mechanism, and potentially also under the cooperative approaches under Article 6.2.[18] This would be particularly relevant for CDM programs where component activities can be added to an existing program, as "new mitigation actions" under the Paris Agreement.[19]

However, transitioning too many CDM activities to the international carbon markets emerging under Article 6 and allowing the use of too many CERs for NDC compliance can generate significant imbalances in international carbon markets and have negative impacts on achieving the overall ambition of the Paris Agreement. One analysis of the CER transition potential estimates that without eligibility restrictions 4.65 billion CERs would be available from registered activities. Such CERs need to be differentiated into what we call "dormant" CERs, i.e., CERs from reductions that have been achieved in the past, but for which no issuance has been requested to date, and future CERs that may be generated until the end of the last crediting period. An additional ~0.7 billion CERs could become available from activities in the process of being validated.[20] India, Brazil, and the People's Republic of China can achieve or nearly achieve their entire NDC targets if they use the CERs available domestically for NDC compliance (footnote 20). This would entail a major blow to global climate ambition. Overall, transitioning this volume of CERs would reduce global ambition from 2020–2030 by about 38% (Figure 1).

[17]   A. Michaelowa, A. Espelage, and B. Müller. 2019. *Negotiating Cooperation under Article 6 of the Paris Agreement.* Oxford: European Capacity Building Initiative. https://www.perspectives.cc/public/fileadmin/user_upload/Article_6_2020_PCG.pdf.

[18]   S. Greiner et al. 2017. CDM Transition to Article 6 of the Paris Agreement. Options Report. Climate Focus. https://www.climatefocus.com/sites/default/files/CDM%20Transition%20Options%20Report%20v2.0.pdf.

[19]   Brescia et al. 2019. *Transition Pathways for the Clean Development Mechanism under Article 6 of the Paris Agreement. Options and Implications for International Negotiators.* Freiburg: Perspectives Climate Group. https://ercst.org/wp-content/uploads/2021/01/Transition_pathways_for_the_CDM_2019-1.pdf.

[20]   Climate Analytics. 2019. *Article 6 Needs Ambition, Not Time Wasting.* Berlin. https://climateanalytics.org/media/carry_over_ca_briefing_11dec2019.pdf.

Figure 1: Impact of Certified Emission Reduction Transition

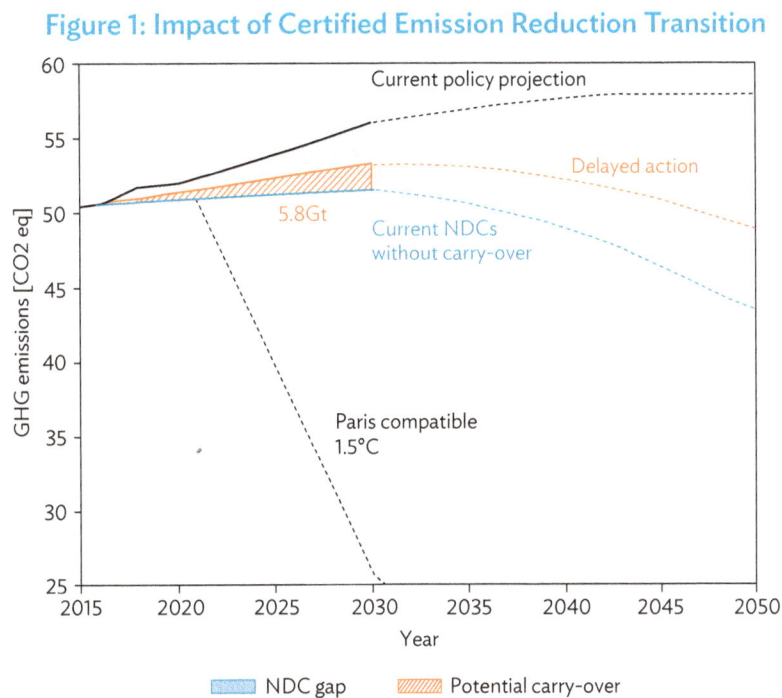

GHG = greenhouse gas, NDC = nationally determined contribution.

Source: Climate Analytics. 2019. Article 6 Needs Ambition, Not Time Wasting.

Given that less than 1 billion of issued CERs remain available on the market,[21] the estimate of over 4.3 billion "dormant" and future CERs becoming available is based on a number of assumptions regarding which CDM activities remain active and are able to request issuance of CERs for emissions reductions achieved in the past and those expected in the future until the end of the crediting period (see discussion in Box 3). Overall, Climate Analytics' estimate seems to be on the high side and should thus be treated with caution. Similar considerations apply for the estimate of 4 billion "dormant" CERs in the period 2013–2020 undertaken by a collaboration of Japanese and German researchers.[22] Another estimate recently published for dormant CERs is much lower at about 2 billion.[23]

21   A. Michaelowa et al. 2021. Volumes and types of unused Certified Emission Reductions (CERs). Perspectives and ZHAW. Freiburg and Zurich. https://www.perspectives.cc/public/fileadmin/Publications/PCG-ZHAW_unused_CERs_PAC.pdf.

22   Ishikawa et al. 2020. CDM supply potential for emission reductions up to the end of 2020. Institute for Global Environmental Strategies, Mitsubishi UFJ Research and Consulting Co., Ltd., NewClimate – Institute for Climate Policy and Global Sustainability gGmbH and Öko-Institut. https://www.oeko.de/fileadmin/oekodoc/CDM-supply-potential-for-emission-reductions-up-to-the-end-of-2020.pdf.

23   A. Marcu, S. Kanda, and D. Agrotti. 2021. CDM transition. CER availability. Bruxelles: ERCST. https://ercst.org/wp-content/uploads/2021/01/20201020-CDM-transition-paper.pdf.

4. Clean Development Mechanism Transition Discussions under the Article 6 Negotiations

The Clean Development Mechanism (CDM) transition has emerged as one of the most contentious issues in the Article 6 negotiations and contributed to the failure to reach agreement on Article 6 at the 24th Conference of the Parties (COP24) in Katowice and the 25th Conference of the Parties (COP25) in Madrid.[24] However, the degree of disagreement on the three key transition aspects varies. The transition of CDM methodologies as well as the relevant components of the international CDM infrastructure (such as the accreditation system) is widely accepted, but the transition of CDM activities less so and transition of Certified Emission Reductions (CERs) is not (footnote 19).

The submissions of Parties' views on Article 6 (as requested by SBSTA 45)[25] to the United Nations Framework Convention on Climate Change (UNFCCC) in advance of SBSTA 46 in June 2017 revealed a wide range of positions regarding the transition of CDM activities.[26] A number of Parties argued for CDM activities to be transitioned into the new mechanism under Article 6.4 and to not lose mitigation activities on the ground and their potential to scale-up due to a change in regime. Some argued that this is critical to the reputation of the Convention while others argued that a smooth transition is necessary to ensure trust in carbon markets.[27] In this context, there were proposals for a blanket transition of all three aspects of the CDM to Article 6 (footnote 27).

Others were open to transitioning CDM activities but noted that this may involve a need for activities to be adapted to the new rules and fully reassessed to determine if they fulfill the new requirements, especially regarding additionality, baselines, and the application of the Article 6 accounting rules (footnote 27). Some Parties argued that the mechanisms defined under the Kyoto Protocol should not continue after the second commitment period. According to this view, the substantive discussion of transitional arrangements should only occur based on agreement on the core elements of the implementing rules under Articles 6.4 (footnote 27).

The positions presented in the submissions from 2017 were maintained during the following couple of years. Issues related to the CDM transition and how to apply corresponding adjustment for the initial transfer from the Article 6.4 registry contributed to the failure of Article 6 negotiations during COP24 in Katowice (footnote 19). However, there was a broader divergence of interests between upper middle-income countries and emerging

---

[24]   T. Forth and F. Wolke. 2020. The Transition Question, Identifying Realistic Numbers for Negotiations on Article 6 *Carbon Mechanisms Review (CMR): Issue* No. 2. Wuppertal: Wuppertal Institute for Climate, Environment and Energy. https://www.carbon-mechanisms.de/fileadmin/media/dokumente/Publikationen/CMR/CMR_02_2020_The_Transition_Controversy.pdf.

[25]   Subsidiary Body for Scientific and Technological Advice (SBSTA) 45th Session. Agenda item 12(a) Guidance on cooperative approaches referred to in Article 6, para. 2, of the Paris Agreement. June 2016. SBSTA Session Documents. Marrakech: UNFCCC. https://unfccc.int/sites/default/files/resource/docs/2016/sbsta/eng/l28.pdf.

[26]   Parties may have adjusted their positions since 2017, but this is the latest public source of country and country group positions and is, therefore, used to highlight the divergence of views.

[27]   W. Obergassel and F. Asche. 2017. Shaping the Paris Mechanisms Part III: An Update on Submissions on Article 6 of the Paris Agreement. *JIKO Policy Paper*. 2017. W. Obergassel and F. Asche. 2017. Shaping the Paris Mechanisms Part III: An Update on Submissions on Article 6 of the Paris Agreement. *JIKO Policy Paper* No. 05/2017. Wuppertal: Wuppertal Institute for Climate, Environment and Energy. https://www.carbon-mechanisms.de/fileadmin/media/dokumente/Publikationen/Policy_Paper/PP_2017_05_Art_6_Submissions_III_bf.pdf.

economies on one side, and least developed countries (LDCs) on the other. A major divide remains between Parties that oppose including any transition modalities and those that call for a full and unrestricted transition (footnote 19). Still other Parties support the imposition of eligibility criteria that would allow the transition of some, but not all registered CDM activities (footnote 19).

The small island developing states (SIDS) and LDCs have negotiated together, stressing the importance of facilitating broad Article 6 participation and signaling the risk of overburdening developing countries by adopting overly complicated rules (footnote 19). Their concerns relate to their CDM experience: many SIDS, LDCs, and African countries attracted minimal investment interest in CDM activities and were unable to reap the benefits of CDM markets when the markets thrived.

There is an indirect link between the CDM transition and the question of allowing crediting from activities in sectors that are not included in the scope of host country NDCs. Several countries and negotiation groups fear this would set a perverse incentive to not broaden the sector coverage of NDCs. On the other hand, country groups consisting mainly of LDCs highlight that the limited scopes of NDCs is due to capacity constraints and that activities beyond the scope of host country NDCs should be allowed for crediting under the Article 6.4 mechanism, where a general additionality test will take place. One proposal is to treat this issue differently under Article 6.2 and Article 6.4, while another is to have a cutoff date to allow for crediting of activities that fall outside the scope of the host country's NDC in the first NDC implementation period only. Accordingly, the eligibility of CDM activities and CERs for transition to the Article 6.4 mechanism could depend on case-by-case assessments of the relationship of individual CDM activities to the NDC of the host country (footnote 19).

To conclude, the preferences of Parties vary, not only on a North–South axis, but also distinctly between developing-country Parties (CDM hosts). The divergence is partly due to differences in stakes that Parties have regarding the portfolios of existing CDM activities that they host, but also due to a general divide relating to principles regarding the use of offset mechanisms. The diverging views are not only an issue for inter-country dialogues, but also have an intra-country dimension. Since corresponding adjustments are most likely to be required, host countries will face internal challenges when developing a strategy for negotiating the CDM transition, given conflicting objectives.

Parties are likely to negotiate for Article 6 rules that allow host countries to decide what CDM activities may transition or not. Figure 2 highlights potential CDM transition goal conflicts and resulting tensions both between and within countries.

Which aspects of the CDM, and what quantities of CDM activities and CERs, will ultimately be transitioned depends on decisions taken by different actors at several layers of the international climate policy regime. The political feasibility of the CDM transition will be reflected in compromises reached during the international climate negotiations, as Parties to the Paris Agreement need to agree on transition criteria, which will be influenced by, but are independent from, the preferences and plans of individual countries for using mitigation outcomes from transitioned CDM activities for NDC compliance purposes. However, national governments also have individual roles to play. Host countries need to decide on what activities they want to transition, and buyer governments need to decide which credit types they want to buy and/or accept in the context of domestic policy instruments. Private sector buyers will also need to decide if they are interested in purchasing CERs from transitioned activities. The owners of CDM activities (primarily companies) will need to decide whether it is worthwhile to go through the formal transition process for their activity and, if not, determine whether it is possible to obtain other types of funding to support continued project operation.

Figure 2: Potential Goal Conflicts in Clean Development Mechanism Transition

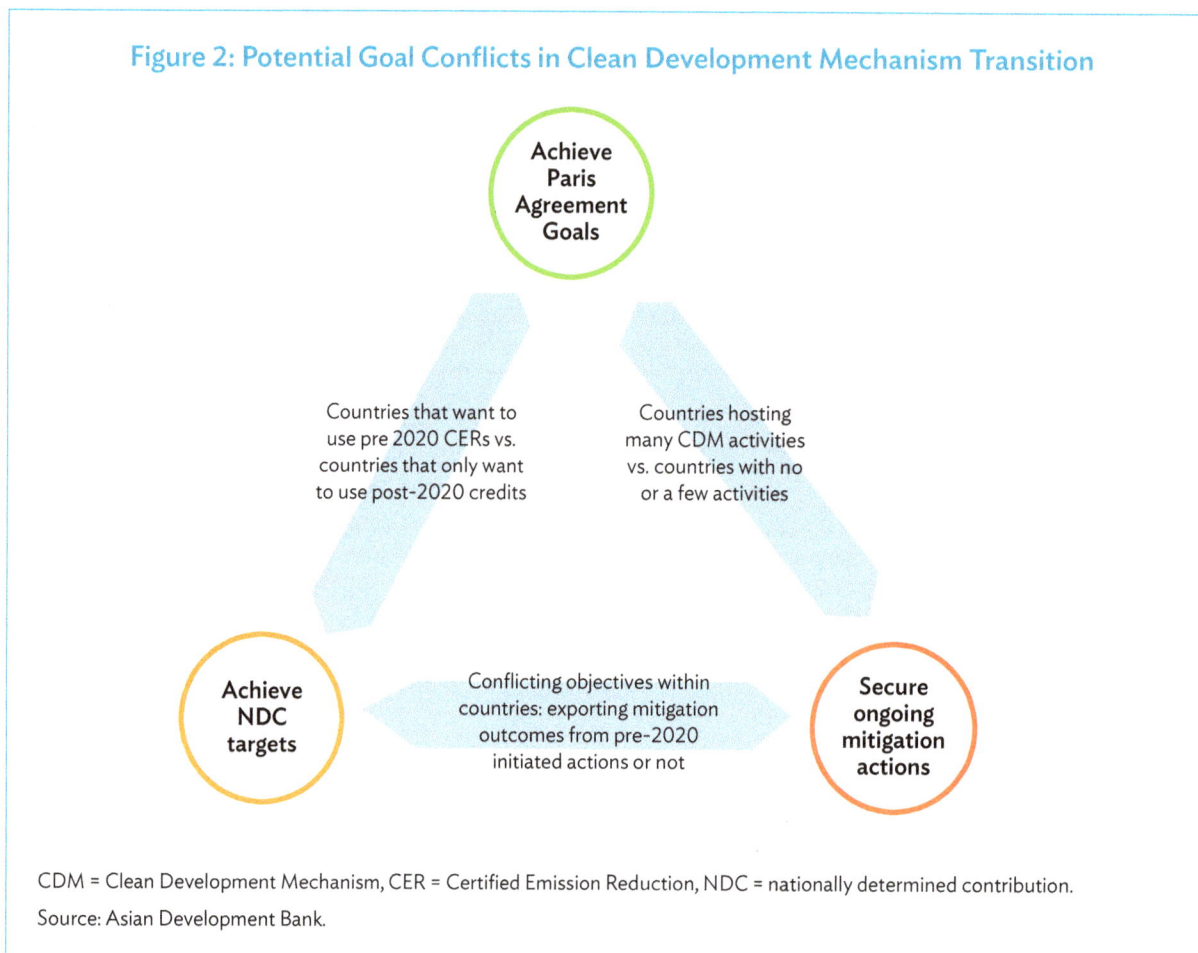

Achieve
Paris
Agreement
Goals

Countries that want to
use pre 2020 CERs vs.
countries that only want
to use post-2020 credits

Countries hosting
many CDM activities
vs. countries with no
or a few activities

Achieve
NDC
targets

Conflicting objectives within
countries: exporting mitigation
outcomes from pre-2020
initiated actions or not

Secure
ongoing
mitigation
actions

CDM = Clean Development Mechanism, CER = Certified Emission Reduction, NDC = nationally determined contribution.

Source: Asian Development Bank.

What is good for a country and, hence, their negotiation position, depends on how different objectives are weighted. On the one hand, countries may value maintaining the trust of owners of existing CDM activities in carbon markets and ensuring that carbon finance from abroad can continue to flow to their mitigation activities. On the other hand, host countries are expected to strive to achieve the targets set in their NDCs, which could imply that issuing Article 6.4 carbon credits from already ongoing (CDM) activities and allowing them to be traded internationally may be challenging if corresponding adjustments must be performed. In the case of Article 6.2 collaboration, which is likely to be started earlier than Article 6.4 activities, these questions may arise in the very near future, as discussions in the context of Article 6.2 piloting exercises show.[28] Thus, host country Parties may prefer rules that allow them flexibility to decide what CDM activities are allowed to transition to the Article 6.4 mechanism. Countries with large portfolios of CDM activities have very high stakes in this issue.

---

[28]   S. Greiner et al. 2020. *Article 6 Piloting: State of Play and Stakeholder Experiences.* Amsterdam: Climate Focus and Freiburg: Perspectives Climate Group GmbH. https://www.perspectives.cc/public/fileadmin/user_upload/PCG_CF_Article_6_Piloting_Dec_2020.pdf.

Box 2: Extending the Mandate of the Clean Development Mechanism Executive Board

Continued Clean Development Mechanism (CDM) operations would require that the CDM Executive Board (EB) remains functional, i.e., that it continues to register CDM projects and POAs, allow new component activities under POAs, and issue CERs for both pre-2020 vintages and for the period after 2020. The CDM EB's competence to continue issuing CERs from pre-2021-vintage CDM activities is uncontested. Regarding resources to support the CDM EB's operation, the accumulated surplus is large enough to cover costs until at least 2023, if not beyond.

The CDM EB has an open-ended mandate for registering CDM activities and issuing CERs. However, in the absence of new guidance from the CMP, the CDM will be unable to issue post-2020 CERs because its technical instructions require that CERs be issued with reference to a commitment period. A group of countries has built its request to not issue any CERs after 2020, and not renew crediting periods starting after the end of 2020, on the basis that there is no third commitment period of the Kyoto Protocol (this also creates challenges for the CDM registry, since CERs must have a commitment-period vintage identifier).

This dilemma has been temporarily solved through a decision taken at the 109th Meeting of the CDM EB to apply provisional registration of CDM activities with the condition that participants need to "acknowledge and accept the risk that it may not be possible for CERs to be issued for the emission reductions achieved." Resolving this issue permanently would require a CMP decision that mandates the CDM EB to register activities after 2020 and issue post-2020 CERs without tying new registrations and issuances to a commitment period.

CER = Certified Emission Reduction, CMP = Conference of the Parties serving as the meeting of the Parties to the Kyoto Protocol, POA = program of activities.

Source: UNFCCC. CDM Executive Board. https://cdm.unfccc.int/EB/index.html.

The Outcome of 25th Conference of Parties in Madrid, 2019

Although there were lines of diverging positions that were not resolved at the 25th Conference of Parties (COP25), following the same pattern as described in Box 2, Parties came closer to a deal than before progress was made in the negotiations on several issues, including issues related to the CDM transition.[29] Parties came close to agreeing to allow CDM activities to transition to Article 6.4 until 2023, provided that they meet the Article 6.4 eligibility requirements (including that the host Party must authorize the transition).

The latest iteration of the Chilean Presidency's text suggested allowing transitioning CDM activities to continue to apply their current CDM methodologies until the end of their current crediting period or 31 December 2023, whichever comes first.[30] After this, they would be required to apply a methodology approved under the Article 6.4 mechanism (see Figure 3 for a tentative timeline). The Supervisory Body would review approved CDM methodologies and methodologies from other market-based mechanisms with a view to adapting them for use under the Article 6.4 mechanism. A6.4ERs could be issued for emission reductions achieved after 31 December 2020 by CDM activities that have transitioned. This likely means that CDM activities only can generate A6.4ERs from the date of their registration as Article 6.4 activities.

---

29   A. Michaelowa, A. Espelage, and B. Müller. 2019. *Negotiating Cooperation under Article 6 of the Paris Agreement.* Oxford: European Capacity Building Initiative. https://www.perspectives.cc/public/fileadmin/user_upload/Article_6_2020_PCG.pdf.

30   Matters relating to Article 6 of the Paris Agreement: Rules, modalities, and procedures for the mechanism established by Article 6, para. 4, of the Paris Agreement, Version 3 of 15 December 1:10 hours.

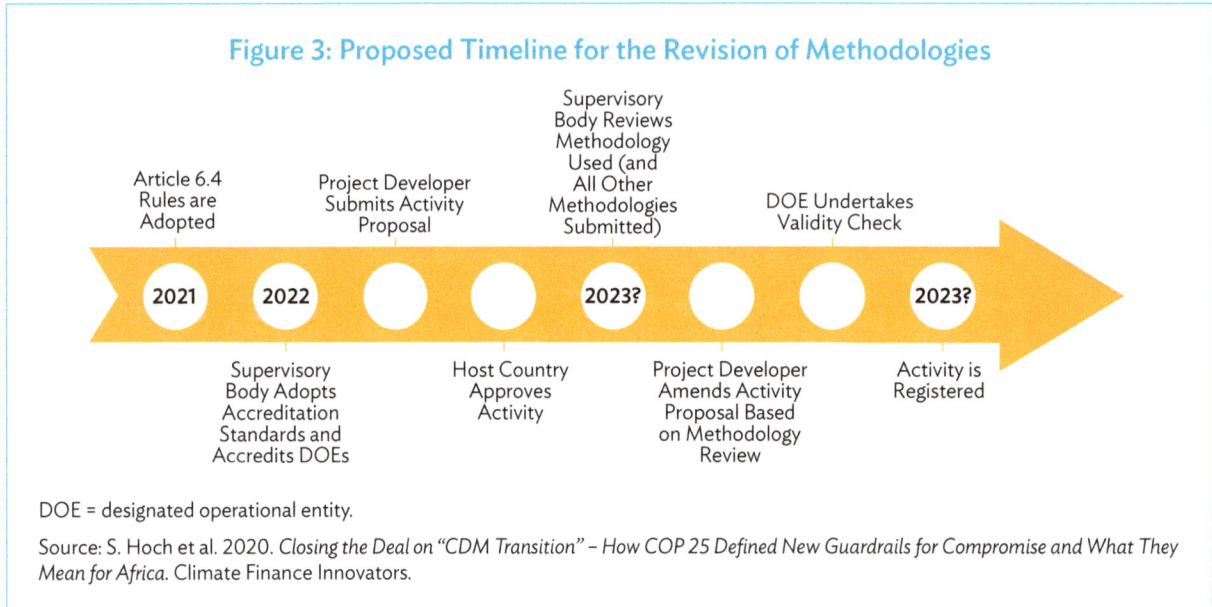

Figure 3: Proposed Timeline for the Revision of Methodologies

DOE = designated operational entity.

Source: S. Hoch et al. 2020. *Closing the Deal on "CDM Transition" – How COP 25 Defined New Guardrails for Compromise and What They Mean for Africa.* Climate Finance Innovators.

In the interest of the African Group, which consists mainly of LDCs, it was suggested that the Supervisory Body should be required to ensure that small-scale CDM activities undergo an expedited transition process.

Following these suggestions, the transition of activities would not undermine the integrity of the Article 6.4 mechanism—particularly due to the requirement that all CDM activities that transition must apply an approved A6.4 methodology by the end of 2023.

Parties remained much further apart on the transition of CERs. The underlying issue is how to ensure the environmental integrity of the Paris Agreement, which relates to Articles 2, 3, and 4 of the Paris Agreement: the objective of the Paris Agreement, the need for ambitious action, the key role of NDCs and their ambition cycle, and the accounting procedures required for demonstrating compliance with NDC targets. Parties have different views on several elements of CER transition, with whether to allow the use of CERs toward NDCs being the most prominent issue. The rationales for not allowing any CERs range from the potential impact on the market price of carbon credits, the risk of undermining the ambition of the Paris Agreement, and the lack of formal support in the Paris Agreement text for a transition. Among those Parties that support allowing CERs to transition, some focus their attention on promoting agreement on transition volumes: whether to allow all CERS to transition or to restrict the volume. Other Parties focus on eligibility criteria or filters, leaving the results with respect to transitioned volumes to whatever they will be (footnote 18).

Other issues relate to how CERs should be managed in relation to the requirement to make corresponding adjustments, the enhanced transparency framework and accounting of NDCs.[31] See Appendix for a summary of proposals and arguments.

The transitioning of CERs per se has no real bearing on the negotiations relating to the rules, modalities, and procedures for Article 6.4.[32] A decision on transitioning of CERs may, therefore, be taken outside Article 6

---

[31]   SBSTA Meeting Draft Agenda item 15 Matters related to Article 6 of the Paris Agreement: Use of Kyoto Protocol units toward NDCs. June 2021. SBSTA session documents. Bonn: UNFCCC. https://unfccc.int/sites/default/files/resource/Inf_note04_Article%206.pdf.

[32]   There is no reference in the Paris Agreement, or in Decision 1/CP.21, that justifies considering CER transition issues under the negotiations of Article 6 rules. See ADB. 2020. Decoding Article 6 of the Paris Agreement Version II.

negotiations, but the CER transition was negotiated under Article 6.4 in Madrid and has been extended to also (SBSTA 2021) being negotiated under Article 6.2 with respect to the requirement to apply corresponding adjustments (section 4.2) (footnote 43). In this context, the main issue is whether CERs issued before 2021 should be allowed to be used for NDC compliance and the focus of the negotiations has been on restricting use by establishing a vintage cutoff date for using CERs.[33] One such proposal would allow all units generated from 2008, while a compromise position was a vintage cutoff of 2013 to 2016. Under the third and final iteration of the presidency text, CERs can be used toward compliance with Parties' NDCs subject to conditions and that such CERs must be used no later than 31 December 2025 (footnote * in the executive summary).

The Chilean Presidency also proposed putting all nontransitioned CERs into a "reserve" to be used in case of future need. Other proposals included requiring that host country Parties would not be required to apply corresponding adjustments for CERs used by 2025 (but CERs transferred internationally for use by another Party would require corresponding adjustments) and that pre-2021 CERs must be identified as such in Parties' reporting in accordance with the Transparency Framework under 18/CMA.1.

The Chilean Presidency's third and final iteration of texts on Article 6 deferred some key issues to a subsequent decision of the Conference of the Parties serving as the meeting of the Parties to the Paris Agreement (CMA), including the vintage cutoff date for transitioning of CERs (footnote 1). Continuing to defer such issues could further delay the implementation of the Article 6.4 mechanism. Figure 4 depicts the transition elements according to the draft negotiation texts from Madrid.

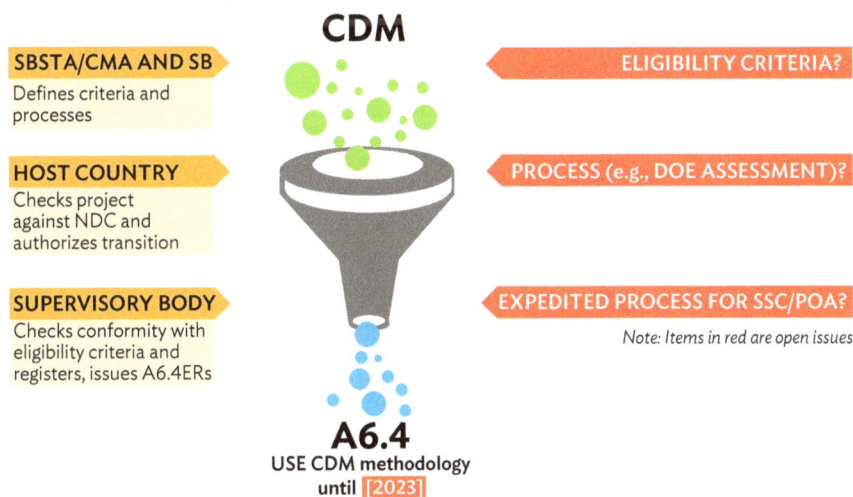

Figure 4: Transition of Clean Development Mechanism Activities According to the 25th Conference of Parties

CDM

SBSTA/CMA AND SB
Defines criteria and processes

HOST COUNTRY
Checks project against NDC and authorizes transition

SUPERVISORY BODY
Checks conformity with eligibility criteria and registers, issues A6.4ERs

ELIGIBILITY CRITERIA?

PROCESS (e.g., DOE ASSESSMENT)?

EXPEDITED PROCESS FOR SSC/POA?

Note: Items in red are open issues

A6.4
USE CDM methodology until [2023]

A6.4ER = Article 6, para. 4, emission reduction, CDM = Clean Development Mechanism, CMA = Conference of the Parties serving as the meeting of the Parties to the Paris Agreement, DOE = designated operational entity, NDC = nationally determined contribution, POA = program of activities, SBSTA = Subsidiary Body for Scientific and Technological Advice.

Source: S. Hoch et al. 2020. *Closing the Deal on "CDM Transition" – How COP 25 Defined New Guardrails for Compromise and What They Mean for Africa.* Climate Finance Innovators.

---

[33]   It should be noted that a vintage cutoff could be defined in terms of the registration of the underlying activity or in terms of the time period in which the emission reduction was achieved. The former definition would be much more restrictive than the latter.

The Subsidiary Body for Scientific and Technological Advice Discussions in June 2021

The discussions under the heading "Clean Development Mechanism (CDM) activity transition to Article 6.4 mechanism" were largely technical and resulted in a list of options presented in the SBSTA Chair's summary, which reveals that the key issues remain largely the same as during previous negotiations (footnote 31):

(i)   **Eligibility of CDM activities for transition to the 6.4 mechanism.** Some Parties argue that all operational CDM activities with a current crediting period should be allowed to transition. Other Parties advocate transition of activities which are either at risk of discontinuing greenhouse gas (GHG) abatement in absence of continued CER revenues ("vulnerable") or meet certain standards and rules to be introduced under Article 6.4.

(ii) **Applying the 6.4 Rules, Modalities, and Procedures to transitioned activities.** There is a suggestion that transitioning CDM activities be required to comply with the A6.4 Rules, Modalities, and Procedures (RMPs) from 1 January 2021. Parties have also suggested that the end of the crediting period or the end of 2023 (whichever comes earlier) should be the deadline for applying Article 6.4 methodologies to transitioned CDM activities.

(iii) **Deadlines for transitioning CDM activities.** Several options have been put forward regarding transition deadlines, including the end of 2023 as the deadline for project participants to express interest in transitioning, the completion of all transitions by the end of 2023, completion of transition by the end of 2025 or the current CDM crediting period of a given CDM activity, or completion of all transitions by the end of first NDC cycle.

(iv) **Transition roles of key stakeholders.** Parties also discussed the role of different stakeholders in the overall transition process. Many Parties highlighted that the host country Parties have the most crucial role in enabling the transition of CDM activities. LDCs argued for the transfer of funds from the CDM EB to the Article 6.4 SB as soon as possible, which is in line with their wish for an expedited transition process.

While the draft decision from Madrid separates the transition of CDM activities from the transition of CERs, but places both under a common section (XI. "Transition of clean development mechanism activities and certified emission reductions"), in the informal dialogues under SBSTA 2021, the transition of CERs was moved to Article 6.2 under the agenda item "Use of Kyoto Protocol units toward NDCs (footnote 31)."

5. Implications Moving Forward

The aim of this chapter is to provide information to policy makers in Asia and the Pacific regarding existing CDM activities globally and in their countries, and what the negotiation texts from Madrid (and the current informal discussions under SBSTA) could mean for them (footnote * in the executive summary).

There are three possible negotiation outcomes regarding the transition of CDM activities (projects and POAs) and CERs into the Article 6.4 mechanism of the Paris Agreement:[34]

(i) Pathway A: All registered activities and issued CERs are eligible to transition.
(ii) Pathway B: Certain limitations are imposed, allowing some registered activities and CERs to transition.
(iii) Pathway C: No activities or CERs are allowed to transition.

The negotiations are sufficiently advanced to safely state that Pathways A and C are not politically viable. The only negotiation outcome that is currently on the table is a set of compromises encompassed in and defining Pathway B. The specifics of the limitations imposed under this pathway are highly debated (Appendix) and the outcomes of detailed decisions will depend on both political and technical feasibility. To identify possible formulations of Pathway B, various scholars have defined transition criteria that provide valuable insights into key issues being negotiated regarding the transition of CDM activities and CERs.[35]

The negotiations in Madrid indicate that POAs and small-scale activities may receive an expedited treatment for transition. With regard to transition criteria, it is possible (as expressed by some Parties at the informal session at SBSTA 2021) that other transition-criteria options such as vintages may be put back on the negotiation table. This is also true for the transition of CERs. This eventuality, for both, is most likely in a situation where the entire or large parts of the final negotiation text from Madrid is reopened, and countries generally return to earlier positions. Accordingly, the spectrum of eligibility criteria that are relevant to transitioning CDM activities and CERs into Article 6.4 is explained in the next section, alongside the most likely negotiation outcomes for each based on the latest negotiation texts.

Transition Criteria and Examples

There are four primary categories of criteria that may be used to restrict the number of CDM activities that are allowed to transition to the Article 6.4 mechanism: restrictions based on the vintage of activities (when they were registered), restrictions based on their scale, restrictions based on their mitigation measures, and/or restrictions

---

[34] Countries can "re-label" CDM activities under Article 6.2, so this discussion is limited to the Article 6.4 mechanism.
[35] J. Fuessler, S. Theuer, and L. Schneider. 2019. Transitioning Elements of the Clean Development Mechanism to the Paris Agreement – *Discussion Paper*, Berlin: German Emissions Trading Authority (DEHSt). https://www.dehst.de/SharedDocs/downloads/EN/project-mechanisms/discussion-papers/transitioning_elements.pdf?__blob=publicationFile&v=2.

based on their host country. These are summarized in Table 2. Although the table has been drafted with the criteria for activity transition in mind, many of these criteria (particularly vintage) are also relevant for transitioning CERs.

Table 2: Potential Bases for Establishing Transition Criteria

Basis for Criteria	Criteria Examples
Based on the vintage of activities or emission reductions. Cutoff based on CDM activity registration date.	Cutoff dates may be established such that only activities registered after a certain date or CERs achieved for reduction after a certain date would be eligible. Dates discussed include 1 January 2013 (start date of the second commitment period under the Kyoto Protocol), 1 January 2016 (which is the cutoff date for CERs under the Carbon Offsetting and Reduction Scheme for International Aviation [CORSIA], or 5 November 2016 (the day after the PA entered into force), but also earlier dates. Criteria have also been suggested related to the activity start date (i.e., the date on which project participants commit to making expenditures for the main equipment or service).[a] Eligibility could also be restricted to activities that would be implemented in response to the new demand from the Paris Agreement and CORSIA.
Based on the scale of potential emission reductions	Efforts to prioritize activities that have significant potential to contribute to transformational change have been discussed. Such motivations can result in restrictions based on scale (small or large) and/or projects versus POAs. POAs have been of particular interest because their impacts can be scaled up significantly by adding CPAs.[b]
Based on type of mitigation measure	Suggestions have included excluding industrial gases (Fluoroform [HFC-23] and Nitrous Oxide [N_2O] from adipic acid); large-scale hydro; activities involving clean coal or coal for industrial applications; and afforestation and reforestation activities. Restricting the eligibility of already-implemented activities to those that are vulnerable has also been discussed.[c]
Based on host country characteristics	Only activities implemented in least developed countries (LDCs), and Small Island Developing States (SIDS) are eligible for the transition, as an example. Only allowing POAs because they are often hosted in poorer countries and are typically regarded as targeting disadvantaged communities and generating larger sustainable development co-benefits has also been discussed.

CDM = Clean Development Mechanism, CER = Certified Emission Reduction, CPA = component project activity, POA = program of activities.

[a] Restrictions on administrative processes in the CDM—such as the start of validation, the date of registration, or the start date of the crediting period—are not appropriate for differentiating between new and already implemented projects, as project participants can often adjust the timing of such processes in response to eligibility criteria.

[b] S. Hoch et al. 2000. Closing the Deal on "CDM Transition" – How COP 25 Defined New Guardrails for Compromise and What They Mean for Africa. Climate Finance Innovators.

[c] T. Day et al. 2019. Supporting vulnerable CDM projects through credit purchase facilities. *Discussion Paper*. Berlin: German Emissions Trading Authority (DEHSt). https://newclimate.org/wp-content/uploads/2020/01/discussion-paper_supporting_vulnerable_CDM.pdf.

Source: Asian Development Bank.

Some of these criteria are more likely than others based on recent progress in the negotiations. However, as seen through the interventions from Parties in the informal discussion under SBSTA during 2021 (Appendix), Parties are still open regarding what criteria to apply. A cutoff based on CDM activity registration date is a practical option, but it does not capture any nuances relating to if the activity is active or vulnerable.

Criteria such as technology type and activity scale are not likely be used to limit the transition of activities, but provisions may be adopted that promote the transition of small-scale projects and POAs. Under the CDM, many small- and micro-scale technologies in the energy sector were included in positive lists, resulting in their automatically being considered additional.[36] The positive-list criteria were often based on a mix of technologies, countries, and consumers. Examples included grid and off-grid solar, offshore wind and marine-based power generation with capacities up to 15 megawatts (MW), rural electrification with renewable energy in countries with less than 20% penetration, and renewable-based power generation with capacities up to 5 MW in LDCs and SIDS. A similar approach using these types of lists could be applied for determining eligibility of CDM activities for transition to the Article 6.4 mechanism. However, given the progress in the negotiations, as seen from the Madrid texts and discussions at SBSTA, cutoff dates are the most likely criteria to go by although other criteria as mentioned in this section could be brought back into the negotiation table by Parties.

The Potential to Transition Clean Development Mechanism Activities Hosted in Asia and the Pacific

The implications of specific cutoff dates for the volume of CDM activities that could potentially transition, as well as basic data related to other eligibility criteria that may apply (such as activity type (project or POA), scale, technology, and type of host country [LDC or SIDS]) are presented as follows.

The information presented in Chapter 4 and the analysis of the impacts of different activity transition eligibility criteria are based on publicly available information from the United Nations Environment Programme and the Technical University of Denmark (UNEP DTU) database. Although the UNFCCC CDM Registry is the primary source of information related to CDM activities, the UNEP DTU database is most widely used when looking at registered CDM activities because it is user-friendly and regularly updated. It is also the database mainly used in the analyses presented in Chapter 4. Other CDM databases have recently emerged, most notably the Institute for Global Environmental Strategies (IGES) database which also is based on information provided in the CDM Project Design Documents (PDDs) available on the UNFCCC CDM website. UNEP DTU is particularly useful because it provides estimates of the aggregate issuance potential up to 2030 for registered activities with renewable crediting periods. However, it does not contain data that would allow assessment of some eligibility criteria, such as vulnerability or more detailed information on unused CERs. For the latter question, this publication provides a detailed analysis based on a recently compiled database (footnote 21).

Clean Development Mechanism Activity Portfolio in Asia and the Pacific

Fourty-four ADB members from Asia and the Pacific are included in this analysis.[37] Among the economies in the region, 21 including those in Central Asia and the Pacific have no registered activities under the CDM.[38] Having said that, the Lao People's Democratic Republic (Lao PDR) and Timor-Leste have one component project activity (CPA) each from a multicountry POA.[39] Table 3 provides the CDM activity portfolio in Asia and the Pacific,

---

[36] J. Fuessler et al. 2019. *Article 6 in the Paris Agreement as an Ambition Mechanism*. Eskilstuna: Swedish Energy Agency. https://www.carbonlimits.no/wp-content/uploads/2019/07/Ambition-Raising-and-Article-6-Final.pdf.

[37] The analysis includes Brunei Darussalam; Hong Kong, China; the Republic of Korea; Taipei,China; and Singapore, which have graduated from regular ADB assistance. Out of these five economies, only the Republic of Korea and Singapore have engaged with the CDM and have a CDM portfolio. More information on classification and graduation of ADB DMCs is available at https://www.adb.org/sites/default/files/institutional-document/31483/om-a1.pdf.

[38] Economies without CDM include Brunei Darussalam; the Cook Islands; Hong Kong, China; Kazakhstan; Kiribati; the Kyrgyz Republic; Maldives; the Marshall Islands; Micronesia; Nauru; Niue; Palau; Samoa; Solomon Islands; Taipei,China; Tajikistan; Tonga; Turkmenistan; Tuvalu; and Vanuatu.

[39] The Lao PDR and Timor-Leste only have one CPA each which is included under the POA 10030: Household energy appliance programme.

including all registered activities in the country level for the 25 countries including Lao PDR and Timor-Leste. The information has been segregated by CDM projects and POAs, with the classification for small-scale and large-scale projects for each, and the cumulative number of CPAs in each county is also highlighted.

A discussion on CPAs is particularly important given a POA could, once registered, add an unlimited number of CPAs without undergoing the complete CDM project cycle which provides many benefits, particularly for less developed countries through the reduction in transaction costs and possibility for a collective approach to monitoring, reporting, and verification (MRV) by utilizing a sampling approach.[40] This means, irrespective of the initial registration date of the POA, CPAs can be added to a POA at much later dates.[41]

As seen in Table 3, a total of 6,476 CDM projects and 153 POAs which represent 701 CPAs have been registered in the region, out of which around 59% of registered CDM projects are large-scale whereas around 88% of registered POAs are small-scale reflecting the differences in size between projects and POAs. The PRC has the largest share of both CDM projects (3,764) and POAs (43) followed by India (1,686 projects and 33 POAs), Viet Nam (258 CDM projects and 13 POAs), and Indonesia (150 CDM projects and 10 POAs). On the other hand, the number of CPAs is highest for India with 234 CPAs, followed by the PRC (143 CPAs), Pakistan (56 CPAs), and Bangladesh (55 CPAs).

Table 3: Clean Development Mechanism Activity Portfolio in Asia and the Pacific, Including All Registered Activities

	ALL REGISTERED ACTIVITIES						
	CDM Projects			POAs			
Country	Number of Registered CDM Projects	Scale of Registered CDM Projects		Number of Registered POAs	Scale of Registered POAs		Number of CPAs Added in POAs
		Small-Scale	Large-Scale		Small-Scale	Large-Scale	
Armenia	6	3	3	–	–	–	–
Azerbaijan	5	–	5	–	–	–	–
Bangladesh	10	3	7	11	11	–	55
Bhutan	5	2	3	–	–	–	–
Cambodia	10	5	5	1	1	–	3
Fiji	3	2	1	1	1	–	3
Georgia	7	1	6	–	–	–	–
India	1,686	1,196	490	33	28	5	234
Indonesia	150	91	59	10	9	1	11
Lao PDR	24	12	12	–	–	–	1
Malaysia	143	114	29	5	4	1	10

continued on next page

---

[40]   UNFCCC. CDM Programme of Activities. Bonn. https://cdm.unfccc.int/ProgrammeOfActivities/index.html. (accessed 7 September 2021).
[41]   A POA has an individual crediting period up to 28 years and has to be renewed every 7 years. Each CPA has a crediting period for either a fixed 10-year period or three 7-year periods. The crediting period for a CPA can, however, not exceed the crediting period for the POA. There are also multicountry POAs where one country is the host country of a POA, but CPAs can be added in other countries. For example, see POA 5962: International Water Purification Programme which has multiple host countries. UNEP DTU mentions the first country, in this case Uganda, as the host country where the POA is registered.

Table 3 *continued*

Country	ALL REGISTERED ACTIVITIES						
	CDM Projects			POAs			
	Number of Registered CDM Projects	Scale of Registered CDM Projects		Number of Registered POAs	Scale of Registered POAs		Number of CPAs Added in POAs
		Small–Scale	Large–Scale		Small–Scale	Large–Scale	
Mongolia	4	3	1	1	1	–	3
Nepal	6	6	–	4	4	–	29
Pakistan	37	16	21	4	2	2	56
Papua New Guinea	10	8	2	2	2	–	3
PRC	3,764	797	2,967	43	40	3	143
Philippines	72	49	23	4	2	2	36
Republic of Korea	91	67	24	8	8	–	27
Singapore	5	3	2	2	2	–	2
Sri Lanka	21	19	2	3	3	–	18
Thailand	144	98	46	7	6	1	15
Timor–Leste	–	–	–	–	–	–	1
Uzbekistan	15	1	14	–	–	–	–
Vanuatu	–	–	–	1	1	–	1
Viet Nam	258	130	128	13	10	3	50
Total	**6,476**	**2,626**	**3,850**	**153**	**135**	**18**	**701**

CDM = Clean Development Mechanism, Lao PDR = Lao People's Democratic Republic, POA = program of activities, PRC = People's Republic of China.

Source: Asian Development Bank using the UNEP DTU Pipeline available at United Nations Environment Programme and the Technical University of Denmark (UNEP DTU). 2021. CDM pipeline; and POA pipeline. www.cdmpipeline.org.

While the total number of registered CDM activities provides a good understanding to the overall role of Asia and the Pacific in participating in international carbon markets through the CDM, many of these registered projects may have ceased operation and may not be currently active. The CDM EB decision to require a request for renewal of a crediting period within a year after its expiry means that dormant projects cannot be put back into life if the crediting period has not been renewed within 1 year from the crediting period expiry date.[42] Globally, of the 7,846 projects and 339 POAs (including 2,723 CPAs as of February 2021), 3,072 projects and 1,111 CPAs have already failed to meet this deadline and have "expired," i.e., they can no longer renew their crediting period.[43] It should also be noted that the vast majority of registered CDM activities with a fixed crediting period of 10 years will have had this period expired by 2022 (footnote 43).

---

[42] CDM Executive Board 100th Meeting Report. August 2018. Executive Board Archives. Bonn/Bangkok: UNFCCC. https://cdm.unfccc.int/Meetings/MeetingInfo/DB/YRCWQVDELB29H4J/view.

[43] L. Lo Re and J. Ellis. 2021. Operationalising the Article 6.4 mechanism: Options and implications of CDM activity transition and new activity registration. *Climate Change Expert Group Paper* No. 2021/02. Paris: IEA and OECD, OECD Publishing, Paris. https://doi.org/10.1787/08ce04ee-en.

Box 3: Factors Affecting Estimates of Potential Activity and Certified Emission Reduction Transition Volumes

Uncertainty of transition volumes for CDM activities and CERs

Estimates of potential transition volumes must be used with care, because performing such estimates requires that several factors that influence transitioning to the new mechanism under Article 6.4 are subject to considerable uncertainty. While one study estimates that the aggregate impact of such factors can reduce CER issuance of up to 40%, the assumptions are highly debatable and not necessarily robust.[a]

Activities that have ceased to operate

With the crash of carbon market and price of carbon offsets that began in 2012, many owners of projects and CPAs struggled to service loans taken to finance their investments, and some projects and CPAs that were under implementation were forced to terminate or suspend operations.

Activities that are operational, but CER issuance is dormant or impossible

Achieving issuance of CDM activities involves transaction costs, including the costs associated with updating PDDs to reflect deviations from the registered versions of documents that occur during implementation and the requirements for achieving crediting-period renewals; monitoring performance; and verification of emission reductions. In the absence of a CER buyer or a sufficiently high CER price, the owners of activities commonly stop issuance. Some of them also stop performing monitoring, which precludes them from performing verification and achieving issuance. Some suggest that while most CDM activities are currently not issuing CERs, they can resume generating CERs if prices increase above current levels. It should be noted that some of this literature is based on interviews done almost a decade ago which thus do not reflect the current situation.[b] Further, their analyses do not take into account the failure of many owners of activities to renew their crediting period in recent years. Also, there is no information on how many activity developers have continued monitoring over the "lean years" of the CDM. In view of key CDM market practitioners, the volume of dormant CERs is heavily overestimated by the recent publications.[c]

CDM = Clean Development Mechanism, CER = Certified Emission Reduction, CPA = component project activity, PDD = project design document.

[a] Ishikawa et al. 2020. CDM supply potential for emission reductions up to the end of 2020.
[b] See for example Ishikawa et al. 2020; Fuessler et al. 2019. *Transitioning Elements of the Clean Development Mechanism to the Paris Agreement*; Warnecke et al. 2017. Vulnerability of CDM Projects for Discontinuation of Mitigation Activities. Assessment of Project Vulnerability and Options to Support Continued Mitigation.
[c] A. Marcu, S. Kanda, and D. Agrotti. 2021. *CDM transition. CER availability*. Bruxelles: European Roundtable on Climate Change and Sustainable Transition (ERCST) https://ercst.org/wp-content/uploads/2021/01/20201020-CDM-transition-paper.pdf.

To segregate the active and dormant activities in Asia and the Pacific, an analysis was undertaken assuming that the CDM activities registered from 1 January 2008 onward should be able to generate credits for at least 1 year from 1 January 2021 and, hence, should have a valid or active crediting period until 31 December 2021. The result of this exercise and further details on the qualification used to create this classification is shown in Table 4.

While all 24 countries that have registered CDM activities currently have active CDM activities, the overall share of CDM activities changes significantly. On the other hand, the POAs remain unaffected as expected given their design to include additional CPAs. However, there is a slight decrease in the number of CPAs as some CPAs within a POA are not active anymore. While a total of 6,476 CDM projects and 153 POAs which represent 701 CPAs have been registered in the region as shown previously in Table 3, only 2,111 (33%) CDM projects and 153 POAs which represent 697 CPAs (99%) are currently active based on the qualification that they should have a valid crediting period until 31 December 2021. For the remainder of the analysis on implications of possible vintage thresholds on CDM activity transition, only the portfolio of active CDM activities from Asia and the Pacific were used.

Table 4: Clean Development Mechanism Activity Portfolio for Active Registered Activities

	ACTIVE REGISTERED ACTIVITIES						
	CDM Projects			POAs			
Country	Number of Active CDM Projects (% of total registered)	Scale of Active CDM Projects		Number of Active POAs	Scale of Active POAs		Number of CPAs Added in POAs
		Small-Scale	Large-Scale		Small-Scale	Large-Scale	
Armenia	1 (17%)	–	1 (33%)	–	–	–	–
Azerbaijan	4 (80%)	–	4 (80%)	–	–	–	–
Bangladesh	7 (70%)	2 (67%)	5 (71%)	11	11	–	55
Bhutan	2 (40%)	–	2 (67%)	–	–	–	–
Cambodia	2 (20%)	–	2 (40%)	1	1	–	3
Fiji	1 (33%)	1 (50%)	–	1	1	–	3
Georgia	4 (57%)	–	4 (67%)	–	–	–	–
India	764 (45%)	545 (46%)	219 (45%)	33	28	5	234
Indonesia	54 (36%)	33 (36%)	21 (36%)	10	9	1	11
Lao PDR	16 (67%)	9 (75%)	7 (58%)	–	–	–	1
Malaysia	26 (18%)	22 (19%)	4 (14%)	5	4	1	10
Mongolia	1 (25%)	–	1 (100%)	1	1	–	3
Nepal	3 (50%)	3 (50%)	–	4	4	–	29
Pakistan	24 (65%)	8 (50%)	16 (76%)	4	2	2	56
Papua New Guinea	4 (40%)	3 (38%)	1 (50%)	2	2	–	2
PRC	995 (26%)	157 (20%)	838 (28%)	43	40	3	143
Philippines	6 (8%)	1 (2%)	5 (22%)	4	2	2	36
Republic of Korea	34 (37%)	30 (45%)	4 (17%)	8	8	–	26
Singapore	1 (20%)	1 (33%)	–	2	2	–	1
Sri Lanka	8 (38%)	6 (32%)	2 (100%)	3	3	–	18
Thailand	54 (38%)	37 (38%)	17 (37%)	7	6	1	15
Timor–Leste	–	–	–	–	–	–	1
Uzbekistan	4 (27%)	1 (100%)	3 (21%)	–	–	–	–
Vanuatu	–	–	–	1	1	–	1
Viet Nam	96 (37%)	46 (35%)	50 (39%)	13	10	3	49
Total	**2,111 (33%)**	**905 (34%)**	**1,206 (31%)**	**153 (100%)**	**135 (100%)**	**18 (100%)**	**697 (99%)**

Color coding: dark green: >75%; light green > 50%; yellow: > 25%; red : <25%; where "%" refers to the % of total registered projects.

CDM = Clean Development Mechanism, CPA = component project activity, Lao PDR = Lao People's Democratic Republic. POA = program of activities, PRC = People's Republic of China.

Notes:

We include the following projects:
1. Projects with 10 years of fixed crediting period should have the start date of crediting period at least from 1 January 2012.
2. Projects with 9 years of fixed crediting period should have the start date of crediting period at least from 1 January 2013.
3. Projects with 3*7 years of renewable crediting period, which were active only for the first 7 years of crediting period, should have the start date of crediting period at least from 1 January 2015.
4. All projects with 3*7 years of renewable crediting period, which already renewed the second 7 years of crediting period.
5. All projects with 3*7 years of renewable crediting period, which already renewed 3rd 7 years of crediting period.

All POAs potentially registered from 1 January 2008 are considered to be active considering their lifetime and possibility to add CPAs.

Source: Asian Development Bank using the UNEP DTU Pipeline available at United Nations Environment Programme and the Technical University of Denmark (UNEP DTU). 2021.

Scale

The overall ratio of large-scale to small-scale projects within the active projects compared to registered projects is around the same (around 57% compared to 59% for registered projects). Figure 5 shows the overall ratio of large-scale to small-scale activities for CDM projects while Figure 6 shows the same for POAs in ADB DMCs. While Armenia. Azerbaijan, Bhutan, and Georgia only have large-scale activities; Fiji, Nepal, Singapore, and Vanuatu only have small-scale activities. The characteristics of projects hosted in India and the PRC also differ considerably, with a large share of projects hosted in India being small scale while the PRC hosts mostly large-scale projects. Such characteristics could be important if they are used as eligibility criteria for transitioning to the Article 6.4 mechanism.

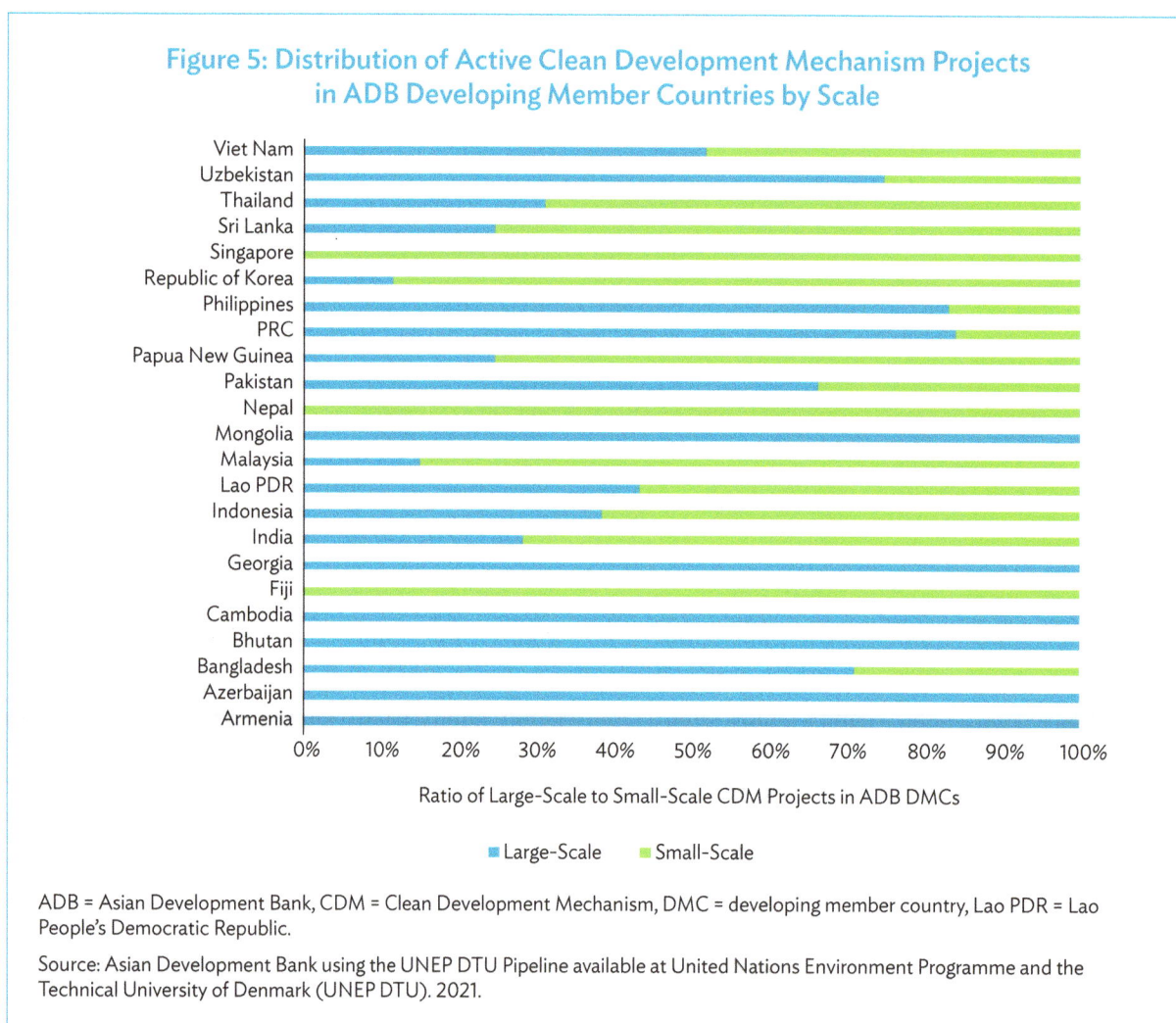

Figure 5: Distribution of Active Clean Development Mechanism Projects in ADB Developing Member Countries by Scale

ADB = Asian Development Bank, CDM = Clean Development Mechanism, DMC = developing member country, Lao PDR = Lao People's Democratic Republic.

Source: Asian Development Bank using the UNEP DTU Pipeline available at United Nations Environment Programme and the Technical University of Denmark (UNEP DTU). 2021.

The overall ratio of large-scale to small-scale is slightly different when looking at the POAs, with a large share of small-scale POAs in ADB DMCs as seen in Figure 6. Out of the 18 DMCs with a POA in Asia and the Pacific, 10 countries only have small-scale POAs while none of the countries have more large-scale POAs than small-scale POAs. Only Pakistan and the Philippines have an equal ratio of large-scale to small-scale POAs.

Figure 6: Distribution of Active Program of Activities in ADB Developing Member Countries by Scale

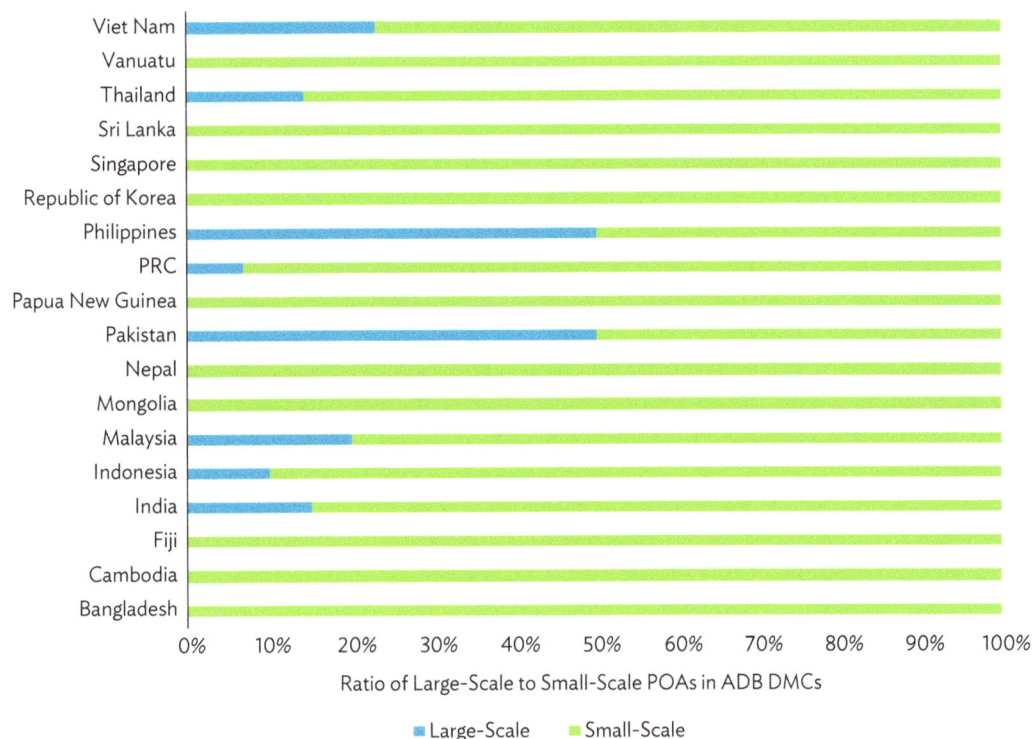

Viet Nam
Vanuatu
Thailand
Sri Lanka
Singapore
Republic of Korea
Philippines
PRC
Papua New Guinea
Pakistan
Nepal
Mongolia
Malaysia
Indonesia
India
Fiji
Cambodia
Bangladesh

0%   10%   20%   30%   40%   50%   60%   70%   80%   90%   100%

Ratio of Large-Scale to Small-Scale POAs in ADB DMCs

■ Large-Scale   ■ Small-Scale

ADB = Asian Development Bank, DMC = developing member country, POA = program of activities.

Source: Asian Development Bank using the UNEP DTU Pipeline available at United Nations Environment Programme and the Technical University of Denmark (UNEP DTU). 2021.

Registration Cutoff Dates

The selection of a registration cutoff date to determine eligibility for transition of CDM activities could have important implications for some DMCs and the activity owners. The third iteration of the Madrid negotiations text and the informal discussions under SBSTA 2021 do not suggest cutoff dates for the registration date of activities that would be allowed to transition to Article 6.4. However, the draft decisions states regarding transition of CERs that "(t)he CDM project activity or CDM programme of activities was registered on or after a date to be determined by the CMA."

It cannot be excluded that cutoff dates for activities may be put back on the negotiation table under a decision by the CMA.[44] It is also possible that there will be no cutoff date defined for transitioning of CDM activities, given that there

44   UNFCCC. 2019. Matters relating to Article 6 of the Paris Agreement: Rules, modalities, and procedures for the mechanism established by Article 6, para. 4, of the Paris Agreement. *Proposal by the President*. Bonn. https://unfccc.int/documents/204686. Para 72: "Project activities and programmes of activities registered under the clean development mechanism under Article 12 of the Kyoto Protocol (CDM) may transition to the mechanism and be registered as Article 6, para. 4, activities subject to: (b) The compliance with these rules, modalities and procedures and any further relevant decisions of the CMA." Matters relating to Article 6 of the Paris Agreement: Rules, modalities, and procedures for the mechanism established by Article 6, para. 4, of the Paris Agreement Version 3 of 15 December 1:10 hours

likely will be a requirement of performing corresponding adjustments for emission reductions verified and issued for re-registered activities. It is nevertheless useful to analyze the impact of cutoff dates as criteria for transitioning of activities because, in addition to activity registration cutoff date being used as a criterion (i) host countries may elect to apply a cutoff date for allowing activities to transition (footnote 43), and (ii) if a registration date becomes an eligibility requirement for transitioning activities, it will also determine the volume of CERs that can transition.

In the following, an analysis based on three dates have been used: 1 January 2008, 1 January 2013, and 1 January 2016. The regional level impacts on CDM activity transition including the associated CPAs that can transition irrespective of their inclusion date as a result of a cutoff date based on POA registration date has been provided in Figure 7.

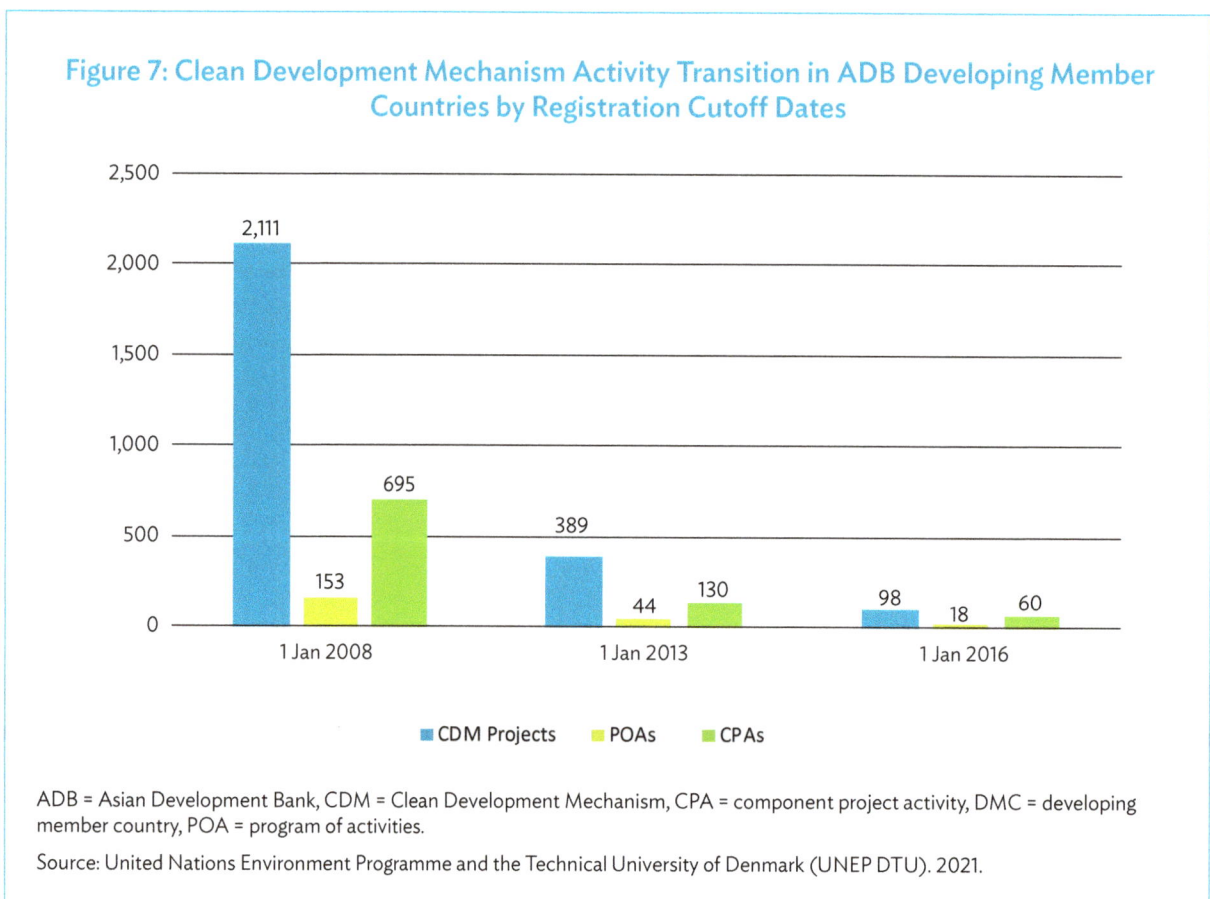

Figure 7: Clean Development Mechanism Activity Transition in ADB Developing Member Countries by Registration Cutoff Dates

ADB = Asian Development Bank, CDM = Clean Development Mechanism, CPA = component project activity, DMC = developing member country, POA = program of activities.

Source: United Nations Environment Programme and the Technical University of Denmark (UNEP DTU). 2021.

Figure 7 shows a significant share of the region's CDM activities have been registered between 2008 and 2013, which means a 2008 registration cutoff would best suit CDM activities in the region as a whole. The difference is less severe between 2013 and 2016. This holds true for both CDM projects as well as POAs and their associated CPAs, which are listed in Figure 7 not as transitioned based on their inclusion date, but on the registration date of the POA. Negotiations on CDM transition do not provide insights on CPAs with regards to CDM activity transition. Having said that, variations exist in the country level with the portfolio of some countries being impacted more than others depending on the various vintages. The impact on the CDM activity portfolio in the country level based on these vintages has been provided in Table 5.

Table 5: Transition Potential Based on Registration Cutoff Dates for Clean Development Mechanism Activities

Country	Transition Potential Based on Registration Cutoff Date with Adopted Criteria for Active Projects								
	Number of CDM Projects			Number of POAs					
	1 Jan 2008	1 Jan 2013	1 Jan 2016	1 Jan 2008		1 Jan 2013		1 Jan 2016	
				POAs	CPAs	POAs	CPAs	POAs	CPAs
Armenia	1	–	–	–	–	–	–	–	–
Azerbaijan	4	–	–	–	–	–	–	–	–
Bangladesh	7	6	4	11	55	8	14	4	7
Bhutan	2	2	1	–	–	–	–	–	–
Cambodia	2	–	–	1	3	1	3	1	3
Fiji	1	–	–	1	3	1	3	1	3
Georgia	4	1	–	–	–	–	–	–	–
India	764	268	71	33	234	9	39	4	31
Indonesia	54	8	3	10	11	1	1	–	–
Lao PDR	16	15	7	–	–	–	–	–	1
Malaysia	26	–	–	5	10	1	1	–	–
Mongolia	1	–	–	1	3	–	–	–	–
Nepal	3	–	–	4	29	4	29	–	–
Pakistan	24	5	3	4	56	–	–	–	–
Papua New Guinea	4	1	–	2	2	1	–	1	–
PRC	995	48	1	43	143	5	6	–	–
Philippines	6	1	–	4	36	–	–	–	–
Republic of Korea	34	5	4	8	26	2	4	1	–
Singapore	1	–	–	2	1	2	1	1	–
Sri Lanka	8	5	1	3	18	2	16	1	4
Thailand	54	11	–	7	15	–	–	–	–
Timor–Leste	–	–	–	–	–	–	–	–	1
Uzbekistan	4	1	–	–	–	–	–	–	–
Vanuatu	–	–	–	1	1	1	1	–	–
Viet Nam	96	12	3	13	49	6	12	4	10
Total	**2,111**	**389**	**98**	**153**	**695**	**44**	**130**	**18**	**60**

CDM = Clean Development Mechanism, CPA = component project activity, Jan = January, Lao PDR = Lao People's Democratic Republic, POA = program of activities, PRC = People's Republic of China.

Note: See Table 5 for definition of what is an active project.

Source: Asian Development Bank using the UNEP DTU Pipeline available at United Nations Environment Programme and the Technical University of Denmark (UNEP DTU). 2021.

The total number of projects and POAs eligible for transition would be reduced drastically (more than 81%) if the registration cutoff date is set at 1 January 2013 compared to 1 January 2008. The PRC and India dominate project registrations in the region. The PRC accounts for 47% of active projects in January 2008, followed by India (36%), but because many of the PRC projects were registered earlier, this relationship reverses if the cutoff date is set for 2013 (India 69%, PRC 12%). The PRC would see its portfolio reduced to 5% while India would see it reduced to 35%. Indonesia, Thailand, and Viet Nam would also see a significant reduction of their portfolios; 11 countries would have no activities to transition if a 1 January 2016 cutoff is applied.

The pattern for POAs is similar, yet less dramatic for the PRC and India. Bangladesh, Cambodia, Fiji, and Nepal host more recent POAs and the portfolios could largely continue with a 2013 cutoff date. The largest shares of active POAs among these DMCs applying a January 2008 cutoff would be: the PRC (28%), India (22%), Viet Nam (8%), and Bangladesh (7%). With a cutoff date in January 2013, the remaining eligible POAs for the same countries would be: India (20%), Bangladesh (18%), Viet Nam (14%), and the PRC (11%).

Adopting a registration cutoff date of 1 January 2016 has drastic implications: the number of projects and POAs in the region that would be eligible for transition would be reduced to a trickle (98 projects and 18 POAs), Bangladesh, India, and Viet Nam would be least affected, each hosting four POAs eligible for transition. Looking at CPAs for the particular POA that is transitioning gives a bit of different picture, but nonetheless highlights that very few CPAs have been included since 2013. In fact, there are only 60 CPAs issued for the 18 POAs that have been registered after 2016.

As discussed, other transition eligibility criteria could be applied. The impacts on DMCs of such criteria are described as follows:

Activity Type

Wind and hydropower represent the largest share of projects registered in DMCs (approximately 35% for wind and 28% for hydropower). Biomass energy projects account for about 8%, followed by methane avoidance projects (roughly 6.5%) and solar projects (roughly 5.5%). The largest number of registered POAs hosted in DMCs involve household energy efficiency (about 24%) followed by methane avoidance (22%) and solar (14%). None of these types of activities are likely to be the subject of transition exclusions. However, some exclusions based on activity type have been discussed, including coal-bed methane, industrial gases, afforestation, and reforestation (footnote 24). Excluding these types of activities would have a minor impact on the number of CDM activities available for transition in the region (Figures 8 and 9). However, the impact on credits that could be transitioned would be large given that some of these projects are particularly large.

Comparing registered and active CDM activities, it is noticeable that biomass energy activities are among the activities where a large number have not been able to continue operation. This is likely a result of their dependence on income from sale of CERs, i.e., these are vulnerable projects. The number of hydropower projects in operation has also significantly reduced, but this is due to these projects having been registered early and with fixed crediting periods that have already expired.

Expedited Processes for Least Developed Countries and Small Island Developing States

The Madrid negotiating text also includes an expedited transition process for CDM activities hosted in LDCs and SIDs. If expedited processes for these countries are adopted, 58 activities (36 projects, 22 POAs, and 96 CPAs)

Figure 8: Types of Clean Development Mechanism Activities (All Registered Activities) in ADB Developing Member Countries

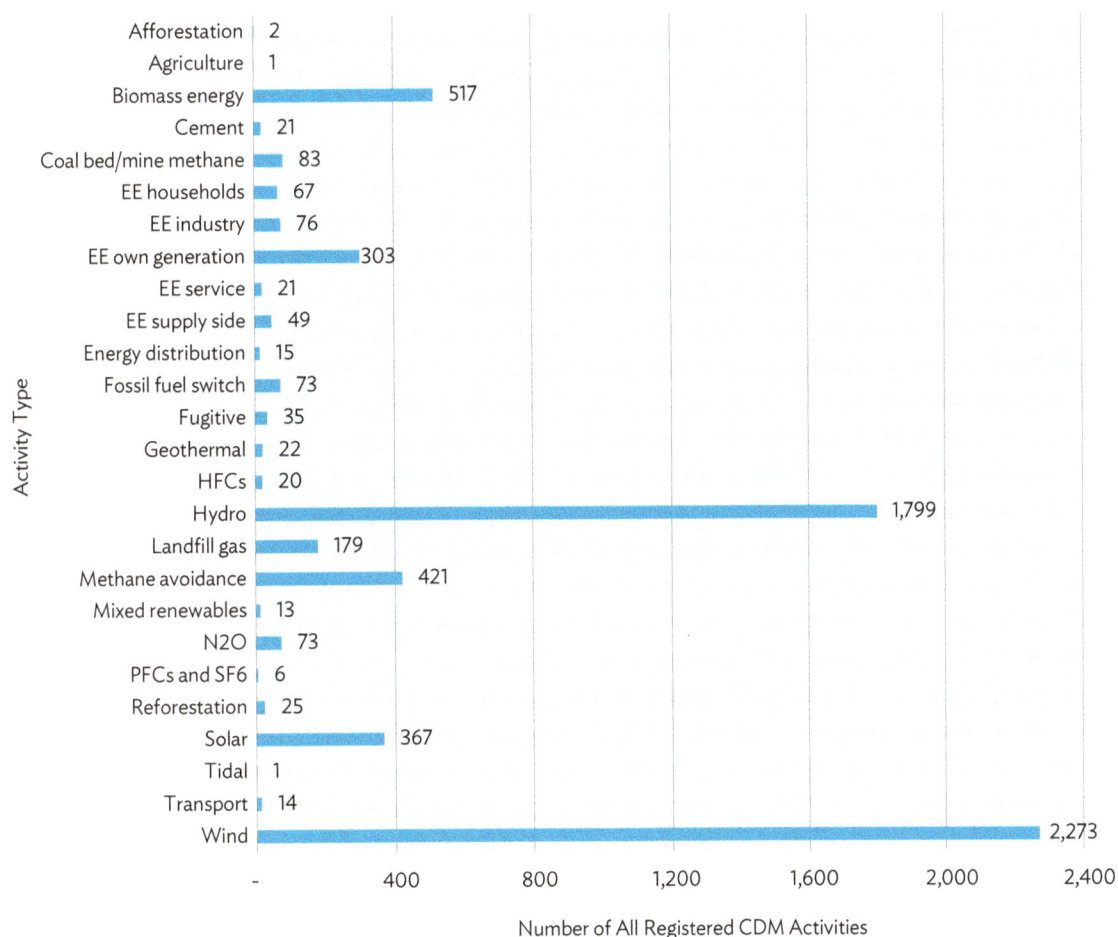

Activity Type	Number of All Registered CDM Activities
Afforestation	2
Agriculture	1
Biomass energy	517
Cement	21
Coal bed/mine methane	83
EE households	67
EE industry	76
EE own generation	303
EE service	21
EE supply side	49
Energy distribution	15
Fossil fuel switch	73
Fugitive	35
Geothermal	22
HFCs	20
Hydro	1,799
Landfill gas	179
Methane avoidance	421
Mixed renewables	13
N2O	73
PFCs and SF6	6
Reforestation	25
Solar	367
Tidal	1
Transport	14
Wind	2,273

ADB = Asian Development Bank, CDM = Clean Development Mechanism, EE = energy efficiency, HFC = hydrofluorocarbon, N_2O = nitrous oxide, PFC = perfluorocarbons, SF6 = sulphur hexafluoride.

Source: Asian Development Bank using the UNEP DTU Pipeline available at United Nations Environment Programme and the Technical University of Denmark (UNEP DTU). 2021.

hosted in ADB DMCs that are SIDS or LDCs and registered as of January 2008 would be eligible to benefit from this. Expedited treatment may also be extended to small-scale activities and POAs. Such provisions could speed up the process of re-registration under Article 6.4.

An expedited process for small-scale activities and POAs, as well as considering special circumstances of LDCs and SIDS would not make a significant difference to the majority of the LDCs and SIDS in the region because they do not host many registered projects or POAs. The difference between a January 2008 cutoff date and a January 2013 cutoff date is small in real terms for both projects and POAs. With a late cutoff date (January 2016), not many activities would be eligible to transition, as seen in Table 6.

Figure 9: Types of Clean Development Mechanism Activities (All Active Activities) in ADB Developing Member Countries

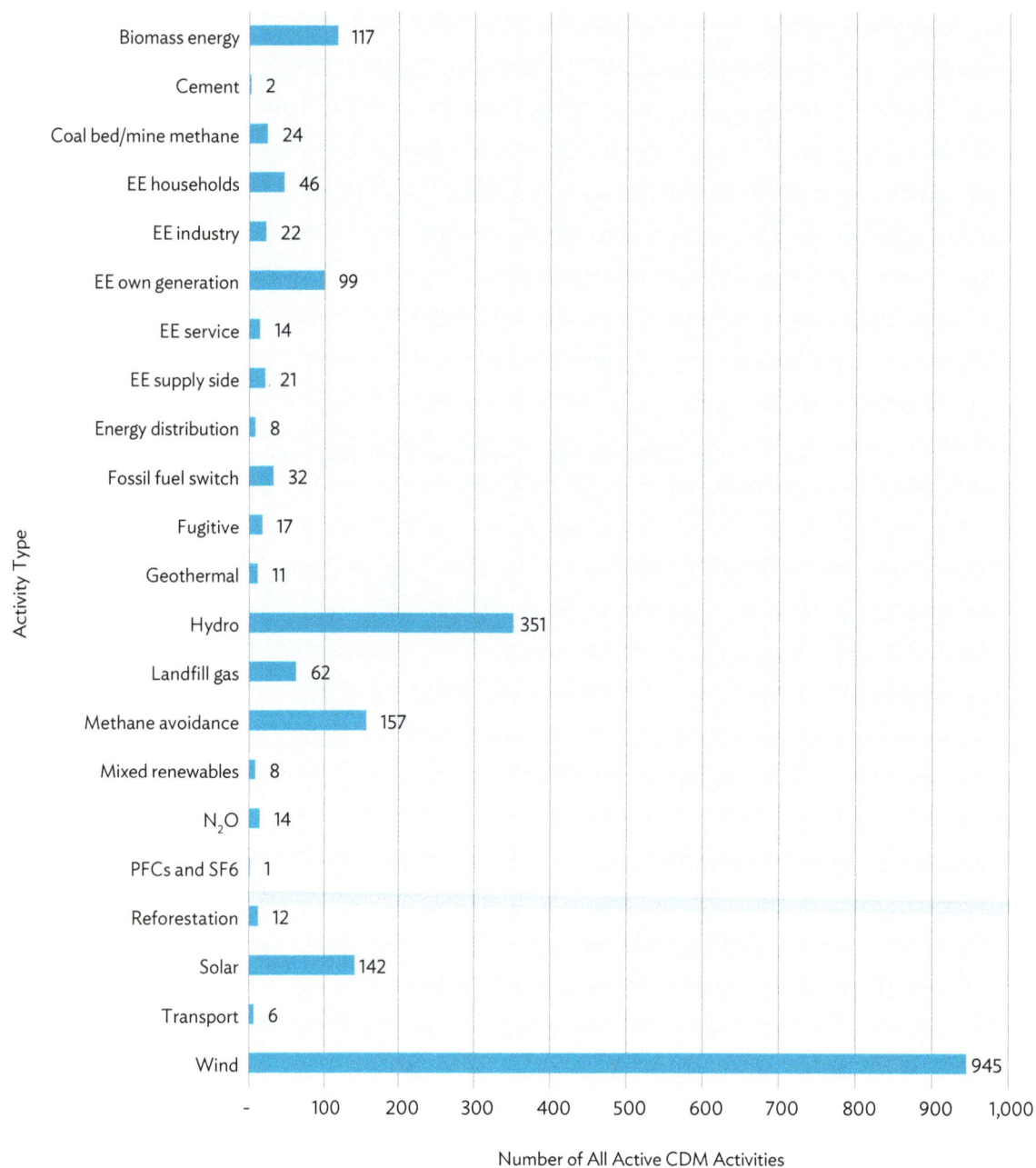

Activity Type	Number of All Active CDM Activities
Biomass energy	117
Cement	2
Coal bed/mine methane	24
EE households	46
EE industry	22
EE own generation	99
EE service	14
EE supply side	21
Energy distribution	8
Fossil fuel switch	32
Fugitive	17
Geothermal	11
Hydro	351
Landfill gas	62
Methane avoidance	157
Mixed renewables	8
N_2O	14
PFCs and SF6	1
Reforestation	12
Solar	142
Transport	6
Wind	945

ADB = Asian Development Bank, CDM = Clean Development Mechanism, EE = energy efficiency, HFC = hydrofluorocarbon, N_2O = nitrous oxide, PFC = perfluorocarbons, SF6 = sulphur hexafluoride.

Source: Asian Development Bank using the UNEP DTU Pipeline available at United Nations Environment Programme and the Technical University of Denmark (UNEP DTU). 2021.

Table 6: Impact of Cutoff Dates on Active Clean Development Mechanism Portfolio in Least Developed Countries and Small Island Developing States

| Country | Number of CDM Projects | | | Number of POAs | | | | | |
| | | | | 1 Jan 2008 | | 1 Jan 2013 | | 1 Jan 2016 | |
	1 Jan 2008	1 Jan 2013	1 Jan 2016	POAs	CPAs	POAs	CPAs	POAs	CPAs
LDCs									
Bangladesh	7	6	4	11	55	8	14	4	7
Bhutan	2	2	1	–	–	–	–	–	–
Cambodia	2	–	–	1	3	1	3	1	3
Lao PDR	16	15	7	–	0	–	–	–	1
Nepal	3	–	–	4	29	4	29	–	–
SIDS									
Fiji	1	–	–	1	3	1	3	1	3
Papua New Guinea	4	1	–	2	2	1	–	1	–
Singapore	1	–	–	2	1	2	1	1	–
Timor–Leste	–	–	–	–	–	–	–	–	1
Vanuatu	–	–	–	1	1	1	1	–	–
Total	**36**	**24**	**12**	**22**	**94**	**18**	**51**	**8**	**15**

ADB = Asian Development Bank, CDM = Clean Development Mechanism, CPA = component project activity, Jan = January, Lao PDR = Lao People's Democratic Republic, LDC = least ceveloped country,POA = program of activity, SIDS = small island developing state.

Source: Asian Development Bank using the UNEP DTU Pipeline available at United Nations Environment Programme and the Technical University of Denmark (UNEP DTU). 2021.

Box 4: Clean Development Mechanism Transition Challenges—Example from Nepal

Nepal has participated in the CDM since 2005 and currently hosts 10 registered CDM activities (6 projects and 4 POAs containing a total of 29 registered CPAs), of which 3 projects have completed their crediting period by end of 2021. All of Nepal's registered CDM activities are small-scale.

As of 2020, CDM activities in Nepal had cumulatively generated over 4.4 million CERs. Of these, 1.7 million (55%) were issued to one POA—the Nepal Biogas Support Program—which is the fourth largest POA globally in terms of issuance.

With a vintage cutoff date of 1 January 2013, only four POAs registered in Nepal would be allowed transition. No CDM activities registered in Nepal would be eligible to transition if a cutoff date of 1 January 2016 were adopted. However, although all POAs in Nepal were registered between 2012 and 2015, 60% of all CPAs were included after 2016. Thus, the example of Nepal illustrates that for POAs setting transition cutoff dates for CPAs based on their inclusion dates would allow the transition of more activities than setting a cutoff date for entire POAs.

An Asian Development Bank case study found that stakeholders (including owners of CDM activities, Article 6 negotiators, and the Designated National Authority) are positive about their CDM experience. However, stakeholders have limited knowledge about post-CDM carbon markets and owners of CDM activities perceive their future prospects for participation as uncertain.

CDM = Clean Development Mechanism, CER = Certified Emission Reduction, CPA = component project activity, POA = program of activities.

Source: Asian Development Bank.

Transitioning Certified Emission Reductions: Impact of Restrictions on the Asia and Pacific Region

Many of the criteria in Table 2 are also relevant for understanding all theoretically possible transition scenarios for CERs linked to the characteristics of eligible activity types and registration date cutoffs. As previously discussed and stated in Box 4, there is a wide spectrum of estimates regarding the potential volume of dormant and future CERs. This section further explores the impact of different CER transition limitations on ADB DMCs.

Certified Emission Reductions Not Sold and Used to Date

Building on a unique database of CDM activities,[45] this section explores how many CERs from CDM activity developers in the Asia and Pacific region have not been used to date. These CERs would thus still be available for transition. The analysis starts with an aggregated analysis on a country level and then looks at activity types.

CERs from Azerbaijan, Bhutan, and Lao PDR have not been used at all to date; 14 countries in the Asia and Pacific region have more than 70% of the issued CERs still available to be used. Only for activities in the PRC, India, Papua New Guinea, Republic of Korea, and Sri Lanka, more than 50% of CERs have been used, as seen in Figure 10.

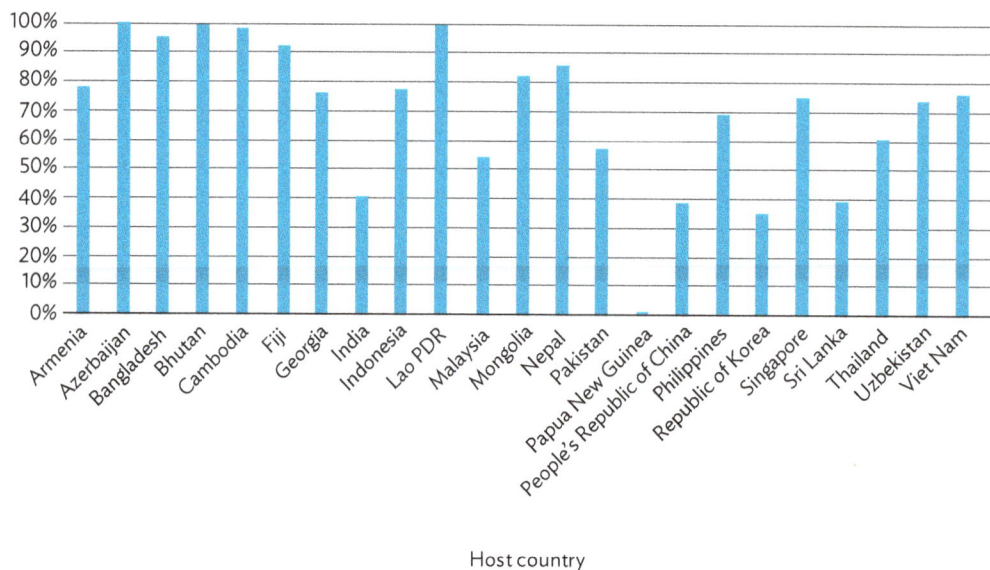

Figure 10: Share of Unused Certified Emission Reductions in Total Certified Emission Reductions Issuances for the Asia and Pacific Countries

Lao PDR = Lao People's Democratic Republic.

Source: Asian Development Bank.

---

[45]   The methodology to derive the volumes of unused CERs and the design of the underlying database is described in A. Michaelowa et al. 2021. *Volumes and types of unused CERs* (footnote 22).

Given that the PRC and India have the majority of share of issued CERs, the total share of unused CERs across Asia and the Pacific reaches 42%, close to India's level of 41% and the PRC's 39%. For the country-specific volumes, see Table 7.

Table 7: Overview of Certified Emission Reductions Issued, Used, and Unused across the Asia and Pacific Countries for All Registered Activities

Host Country	Issued CERs	Used CERs	Unused CERs	Share of Unused CERs in Total CERs issued
Armenia	135,642	29,897	105,745	78%
Azerbaijan	53,070	–	53,070	100%
Bangladesh	11,869,456	519,664	11,349,792	96%
Bhutan	1,866,791	6,855	1,859,936	100%
Cambodia	7,462,596	128,643	7,333,953	98%
Fiji	268,380	19,729	248,651	93%
Georgia	1,531,865	365,049	1,166,816	76%
India	263,009,539	156,240,650	106,768,889	41%
Indonesia	37,533,458	8,386,865	29,146,593	78%
Lao PDR	3,570,068	15,393	3,554,675	100%
Malaysia	13,495,037	6,213,952	7,281,085	54%
Mongolia	1,437,132	253,140	1,183,992	82%
Nepal	4,576,647	644,869	3,931,778	86%
Pakistan	9,905,795	4,227,919	5,677,876	57%
Papua New Guinea	318,029	315,976	2,053	1%
PRC	1,113,137,843	680,296,084	432,841,759	39%
Philippines	4,085,950	1,259,581	2,826,369	69%
Republic of Korea	183,692,189	119,370,203	64,321,986	35%
Singapore	55,507	14,000	41,507	75%
Sri Lanka	1,345,160	821,764	523,396	39%
Thailand	14,999,086	5,865,655	9,133,431	61%
Uzbekistan	17,860,915	4,658,246	13,202,669	74%
Viet Nam	26,320,923	6,224,152	20,096,771	76%
Total	**1,720,181,044**	**996,032,080**	**724,148,964**	**42%**

CER = certified emission reduction, Lao PDR = Lao People's Democratic Republic, PRC = People's Republic of China.

Source: Asian Development Bank.

For POAs, the share of unused CERs is much higher than for projects, reaching 90% on average (Table 8). This is due to the fact that POAs started much later than projects and thus were unable to benefit from high CER demand pre-2012. The PRC and India perform better than average, with 85% and 87%, respectively, as seen in Table 8.

Table 8: Overview of Certified Emission Reductions Issued, Used, and Unused Differentiated by Projects and Program of Activities

Host Country	CDM Projects			POAs		
	Issued CERs	Used CERs	Unused CERs	Issued CERs	Used CERs	Unused CERs
Armenia	135,642	29,897	105,745	–	–	–
Azerbaijan	53,070	–	53,070	–	–	–
Bangladesh	8,015,357	52,777	7,962,580	3,854,099	466,887	3,387,212
Bhutan	1,866,791	6,855	1,859,936	–	–	–
Cambodia	7,462,596	128,643	7,333,953		–	–
Fiji	241,764	19,729	222,035	26,616	–	26,616
Georgia	1,531,865	365,049	1,166,816	–	–	–
India	257,020,626	155,470,845	101,549,781	5,988,913	769,805	5,219,108
Indonesia	37,431,284	8,386,865	29,044,419	102,174	–	102,174
Lao PDR	3,570,068	15,393	3,554,675	–	–	–
Malaysia	13,495,037	6,213,952	7,281,085		–	–
Mongolia	1,040,776	253,140	787,636	396,356	–	396,356
Nepal	1,979,187	374,443	1,604,744	2,597,460	270,426	2,327,034
Pakistan	9,905,795	4,227,919	5,677,876			
Papua New Guinea	318,029	315,976	2,053		–	–
PRC	1,108,762,787	679,625,193	429,137,594	4,375,056	670,891	3,704,165
Philippines	3,891,288	1,259,581	2,631,707	194,662	–	194,662
Republic of Korea	183,675,039	119,353,396	64,321,643	17,150	16,807	343
Singapore	55,507	14,000	41,507		–	–
Sri Lanka	1,264,253	821,764	442,489	80,907	–	80,907
Thailand	14,724,446	5,865,042	8,859,404	274,640	613	274,027
Uzbekistan	17,860,915	4,658,246	13,202,669	–	–	–
Viet Nam	24,632,067	6,224,152	18,407,915	1,688,856	–	1,688,856
Total	**1,699,435,261**	**993,821,756**	**705,613,505**	**20,745,783**	**2,210,324**	**18,535,459**

CDM = Clean Development Mechanism, CER = certified emission reduction, Lao PDR = Lao People's Democratic Republic, POA = program of activities, PRC = People's Republic of China.

Source: Asian Development Bank.

Figure 11 depicts the share of unused CERs from individual project types in total unused CERs in the Asia and Pacific region. Wind (21.2% of total unused CERs), hydro (18.8% of total unused CERs), hydrofluorocarbon (HFCs, 13.7% of total unused CERs) and nitrous oxide (N_2O, 10.6% of total unused CERs) activities constitute the major share of unused CERs.

Figure 12 depicts the share of unused CERs in total CERs issued from individual project types in the Asia and Pacific region. Hybrid renewables (100%), energy distribution (99.3%), energy efficiency (EE) service (97.9%), transport (89.2%), EE households (89.2%), mixed renewables (81.9%), fugitive (79.8%), EE supply side (79.7%), and geothermal (74.8%) were the project types with the lowest success in selling CERs. The most successful categories were industrial gas projects, solar, and tidal energy.

Figure 11: Share of Unused Certified Emission Reductions for Each Activity Type in Total Unused Certified Emission Reductions in the Asia and Pacific Region

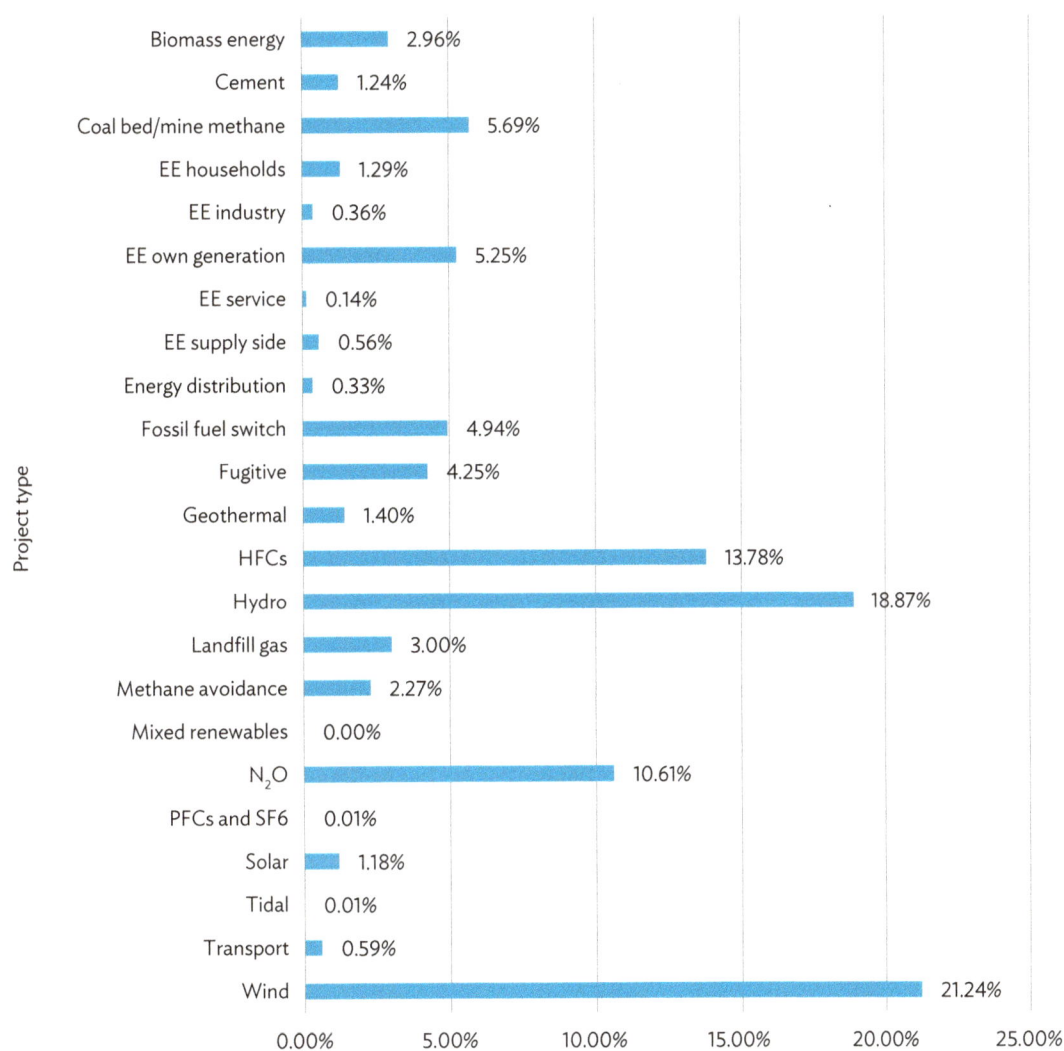

Project type	Share
Biomass energy	2.96%
Cement	1.24%
Coal bed/mine methane	5.69%
EE households	1.29%
EE industry	0.36%
EE own generation	5.25%
EE service	0.14%
EE supply side	0.56%
Energy distribution	0.33%
Fossil fuel switch	4.94%
Fugitive	4.25%
Geothermal	1.40%
HFCs	13.78%
Hydro	18.87%
Landfill gas	3.00%
Methane avoidance	2.27%
Mixed renewables	0.00%
N_2O	10.61%
PFCs and SF6	0.01%
Solar	1.18%
Tidal	0.01%
Transport	0.59%
Wind	21.24%

EE = energy efficiency, HFC = hydrofluorocarbon, N_2O = nitrous oxide, PFC = perfluorocarbons, SF6 = sulphur hexafluoride.

Source: Asian Development Bank.

Vintage cutoff dates, wind activities are the largest activity type when there is no cutoff or a cutoff from 2008, with 153 million unused CERs in total and 139 million CERs from 2008. For cutoff with registration dates from 2013, hydro activities come to the fore with 19.6 million unused CERs and finally, for cutoff with registration dates from 2016, EE household activities become relevant with 1.3 million unsold CERs. As can be seen in Figure 13, wind and hydro projects are the most important sources of unused CERs. However, their share falls sharply when a later cutoff date is set and activities such as EE households and solar gain importance.

Figure 12: Share of Unused Certified Emission Reductions in Total Certified Emission Reductions Issued for Each Activity Type in the Asia and Pacific Region

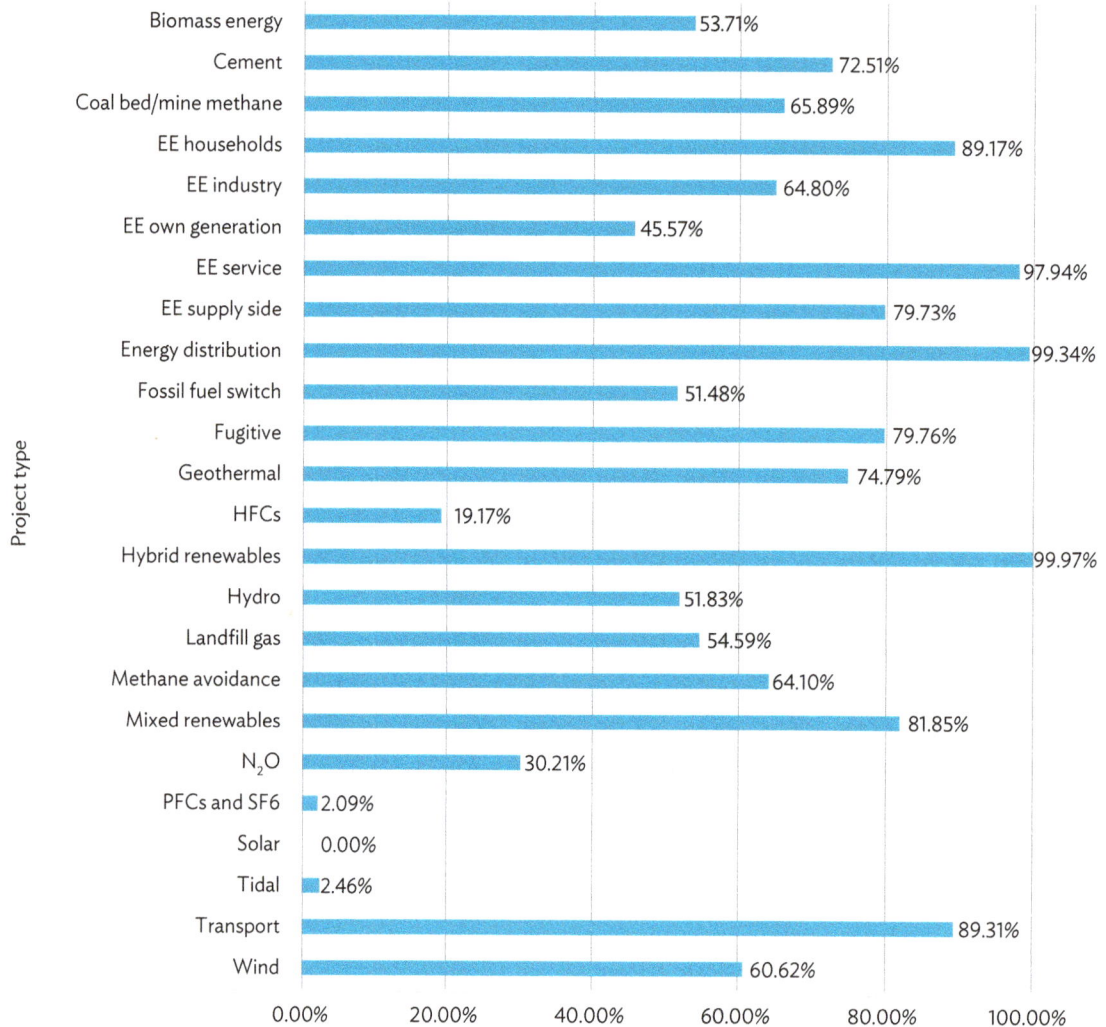

Project type	Share
Biomass energy	53.71%
Cement	72.51%
Coal bed/mine methane	65.89%
EE households	89.17%
EE industry	64.80%
EE own generation	45.57%
EE service	97.94%
EE supply side	79.73%
Energy distribution	99.34%
Fossil fuel switch	51.48%
Fugitive	79.76%
Geothermal	74.79%
HFCs	19.17%
Hybrid renewables	99.97%
Hydro	51.83%
Landfill gas	54.59%
Methane avoidance	64.10%
Mixed renewables	81.85%
N$_2$O	30.21%
PFCs and SF6	2.09%
Solar	0.00%
Tidal	2.46%
Transport	89.31%
Wind	60.62%

EE = energy efficiency, HFC = hydrofluorocarbon, N$_2$O = nitrous oxide, PFC = perfluorocarbons, SF6 = sulphur hexafluoride.
Source: Asian Development Bank.

The next step is a look at how unused CER shares of specific countries change with different registration cutoff dates. With 2008 and 2013 cutoffs, the PRC continues to be the leader with the largest unsold CERs, although the share of unused CERs declines considerably under the 2013 cutoff (about a 30% decline). A 2016 cutoff would render all CERs from the PRC ineligible for NDC compliance markets, as only one activity was registered in the PRC after 2016 and this project has no CER issuances. As a result, project developers in the PRC would advocate for a cutoff date not later than 2008.

Figure 13: Top 10 Project Types with Unused Certified Emission Reductions by Different Activity Registration Dates in the Asia and Pacific Region

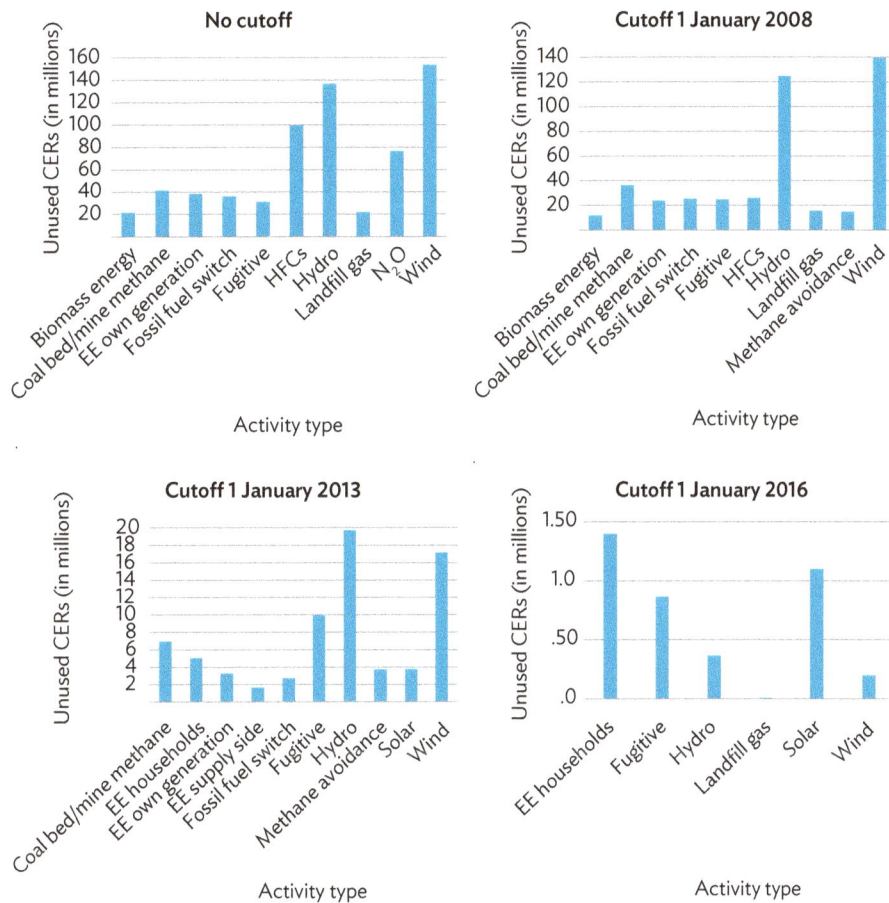

CER = certified emission reduction, EE = energy efficiency, HFC = hydrofluorocarbon, N_2O = nitrous oxide.

Note: With cutoff date after 2016, only six project types were left. Note the strong variation of the y-axis scale (amount of CERs) when comparing the figures. Please also note that different project types dominate the portfolio with a different registration cutoff date of 2020.

Source: Asian Development Bank.

For India, with a cutoff for project registration in 2008, around 50% of the unused CERs become ineligible for use in NDC compliance markets. When applying 2013 and 2016 cutoffs, 13 million CERs (for 2013) and approximately 1 million CERs (for 2016) are still eligible in a post-2020 period. Therefore, India continues to remain important as a host country across all registration date thresholds as opposed to the PRC. Bangladesh gains importance as a host country when a 2016 cutoff is imposed, with more than 2 million CERs being eligible for NDC compliance markets. Therefore, developers in Bangladesh would argue for a later cutoff date.

Figure 14: Main Host Countries of Activities with Unused Certified Emission Reductions According to Different Activity Registration Dates

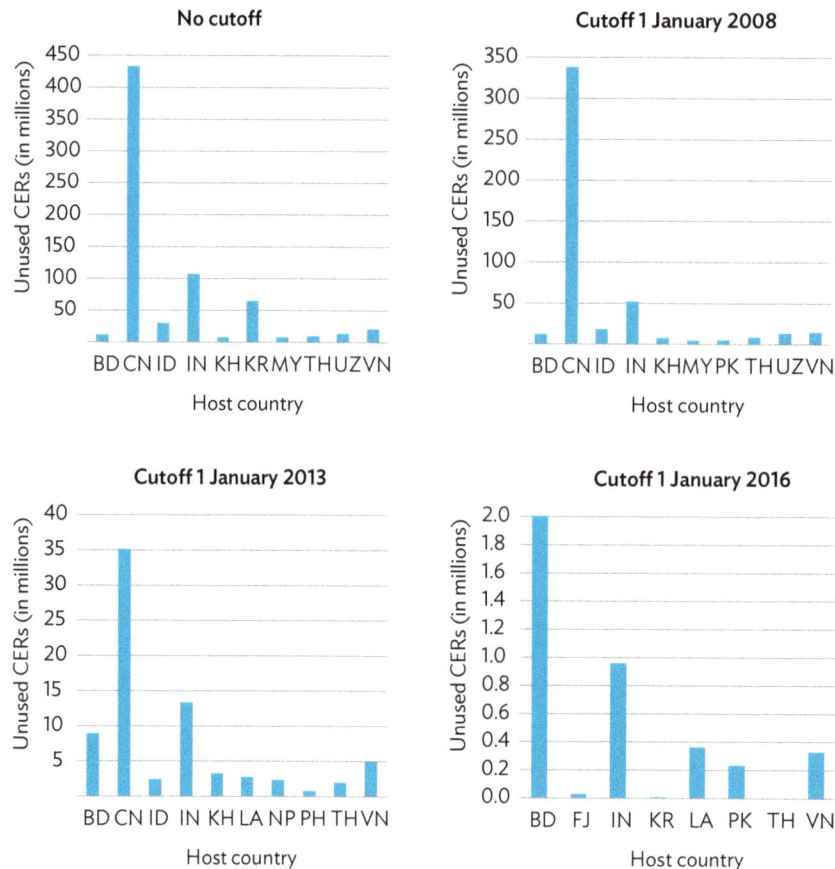

BD = Bangladesh, CER = certified emission reduction, CN = People's Republic of China, FJ = Fiji, ID = Indonesia, IN = India, KH = Cambodia, KR = Republic of Korea, LA = Lao People's Democratic Republic, MY = Malaysia, NP = Nepal, PH = Philippines, PK = Pakistan, TH = Thailand, UZ = Uzbekistan, VN = Viet Nam. With cutoff date after 2016, only eight host countries were left. Note the strong variation of the y-axis scale (amount of CERs) when comparing the figures.

Source: Asian Development Bank.

Cutoff Dates for Program of Activities

Parties may agree to the transition of CERs under CPA inclusion cutoff dates instead of transition of CERs depending on the registration date of the associated POA. This has impacts on the available CERs for transition as although a POA might have been registered in 2009, well before the 2013 cutoff date, CPAs can be included well after the 2013 cutoff date which might have then issued CERs. The impact of a shift to a CPA inclusion date is shown in Table 9. Note that the analysis in this table refers to issued, not unused CERs, so it overestimates the transition potential.

Table 9: Total Certified Emission Reductions Transition Scenario Based on Program of Activities Registration Date versus Component Project Activity Inclusion Date

Country	Potential Transition of Issued CERs Based on Registration Cutoff Date of CDM POAs			Potential Transition of Issued CERs Based on Inclusion Cutoff Date of CPAs		
	POAs (in kCERs)			CPAs (in kCERs)		
	1 Jan 2008	1 Jan 2013	1 Jan 2016	1 Jan 2008	1 Jan 2013	1 Jan 2016
Bangladesh	3,816	1,504	1,504	3,816	3,673	2,976
Cambodia	–	–	–	32	32	32
Fiji	27	27	27	27	27	27
India	6,162	165	64	6,002	3,065	1,465
Indonesia	102	–	–	102	15	–
Lao PDR	–	–	–	4	4	4
Mongolia	396	–	–	396	144	144
Nepal	2,636	2,636	–	2,636	2,636	225
PRC	4,368	–	–	4,368	4,277	–
Philippines	195	–	–	195	186	167
Republic of Korea	17	–	–	17	10	10
Sri Lanka	81	81	–	81	81	12
Thailand	275	–	–	275	185	–
Viet Nam	1,721	221	221	1,721	1,560	251
Total	**19,796**	**4,634**	**1,816**	**19,672**	**15,985**	**5,313**

CDM = Clean Development Mechanism, CER = certified emission reduction, CPA = component project activity, Jan = January, kCER = thousand of certified emission reduction, Lao PDR = Lao People's Democratic Republic, POA = program of activity, PRC = People's Republic of China.

Source: Asian Development Bank.

Looking at cutoff dates from the point of view of inclusion of CPAs provides interesting implications.[46] At the regional level, up to 11 million additional CERs (around 4 million CERs can transition when total CERs based on activity cutoff date is used for 2013) can transition if CPA inclusion dates are used as criterion compared to using a POA registration date under a 2013 cutoff, and up to 3.5 million CERs can transition based on a 2016 cutoff date. In fact, of the 14 countries with a POA portfolio in Asia and the Pacific, all countries are better off with a CPA inclusion date as a criterion either under a 2013 vintage or a 2016 vintage.

---

[46] It is reasonable to expect that available CERs under CPA inclusion dates will be equal or higher than those under POA registration given CPAs can only succeed a POA. This is seen for all countries except for India in 2008. This may be because of multicountry POAs listed to be hosted in India by the UNEP DTU database, but CPAs also being issued elsewhere such as POA 7997: BioLite Improved Cook Stoves Programme hosted in India, Kenya, and Uganda, although the UNEP DTU registry only lists India as the host country.

6. Host Country Considerations and Challenges in the Context of Clean Development Mechanism Transition

Authorizing Article 6 versus Clean Development Mechanism Designated National Authority Functions: A Higher Degree of Responsibility

One might assume that Clean Development Mechanism (CDM) activities will transition to the new Article 6.4 mechanism, i.e., from one United Nations Framework Convention on Climate Change (UNFCCC) mechanism with centralized oversight to another. However, it will also be possible to transition de-registered CDM activities to cooperative approaches implemented under Article 6.2 as the countries engaged in those can freely decide to engage in transitioned CDM activities. As long as the Article 6.2 requirements on reporting, review, and accounting are followed, transitions of this type do not require international approval.[47] Host country responsibilities may differ, however, depending on what type of market mechanism a CDM activity is intended to transition to under an Article 6.2 collaboration.

Under the CDM, the host country's Designated National Authority (DNA) issued a Letter of Approval (LOA) for a project or a program of activities (POA), including an authorization of the participants. As host countries had no quantitative commitments under the Kyoto Protocol, the approval of CDM activities only meant confirming that participation was voluntary and contributed domestically to sustainable development. There was no Kyoto compliance risk for the host country. Hence, most countries were willing to deliver LOAs without implementing complicated approval processes. There were exceptions, though, like in Malaysia or Uruguay where countries wanted to ensure sustainable development co-benefits of the activity.[48]

Since all Parties to the Paris Agreement have mitigation commitments, authorizing activities to participate in Article 6 mechanisms will become more relevant for host countries. Assessing the activity's contribution to sustainable development will remain important but will not be the only aspect. Since countries are expected to report to the UNFCCC[49] ex post on how mitigation actions contribute to the nationally determined contribution (NDC) and are consistent with sustainable development and environmental integrity requirements, host countries will have to regulate Article 6 implementation domestically, adopting not just procedural rules, but also content, for example, ensuring that transitioning activities comply with national additionality requirements (footnote 47). This will be

---

[47] M. Unger. 2019. *Host Country Authorizations under Article 6 Paris Agreement: Developments After COP 24 (Katowice)*. Berlin: Atlas Environmental Law Advisory. https://www.carbon-mechanisms.de/fileadmin/media/dokumente/Publikationen/Studie/Studie_2019_ATLAS_Host_Country_Authorizations_Art_6_eng.pdf.

[48] A. Michaelowa. 2005. Creating the foundations for host country participation in the CDM: experiences and challenges in CDM capacity building, in F. Yamin, ed. *Climate change and carbon markets. A handbook of emission reduction mechanisms*. London. Earthscan. pp. 305–320.

[49] Subsidiary Body for Scientific and Technological Advice (SBSTA) 45th Session. Agenda item 12(a) Guidance on cooperative approaches referred to in Article 6, para. 2, of the Paris Agreement. June 2016. SBSTA Session Documents. Marrakech: UNFCCC. https://unfccc.int/sites/default/files/resource/docs/2016/sbsta/eng/l28.pdf.

particularly true for activities transitioning to Article 6.2 mechanisms given the need for corresponding adjustments to the host country's NDC.[50]

Under both Articles 6.2 and 6.4, the host country will be engaged in the transition at two levels. First, there is the assessment of whether to authorize the activity for re-registration. The host country must apply its own criteria, which may exceed those in the international rules. Such additional criteria could either add stringency to the international eligibility criteria or introduce new eligibility criteria not covered by the international rules, or both (footnote 43). For those activities that will be granted transition authorization, there will be administrative tasks related to confirming that the activity has been de-registered from the CDM if required by the Article 6 rulebook and communicating the authorization to the Article 6 governing authority.

Whereas CDM DNAs typically were located within ministries of environment and had support from an advisory or assessing committee, the body for Article 6 authorization may need stronger coordination with different ministries, either through a clear and comprehensive policy for authorization, or if a bottom–up approach to eligible mitigation actions is preferred, a process that incorporates sector ministries and agencies. It also should be linked to the NDC implementation process (footnote 50).

Domestic governance of Article 6 will be important in the transition process where coordination is needed within host Parties, especially if their institutions responsible for operational aspects of the CDM and the Article 6 mechanism are not the same. Coordination with the domestic body that coordinates monitoring and tracking of the NDC is also necessary (footnote 43).

Box 5: Preliminary Responsibilities of the Host Country Under Article 6.4

Some of the responsibilities associated with authorizing Article 6 activities will be similar to those of Clean Development Mechanism designated national authorities, but there will be new responsibilities as well. Host country responsibilities under Article 6.4 are likely to include:

(i)   The designation of a national authority for the Article 6.4 mechanism and informing the United Nations Framework Convention on Climate Change Secretariat about the designation.
(ii) A public announcement of how participation in the Article 6.4 mechanism will contribute to sustainable development in the national context.
(iii) The submission of publicly available information to the Supervisory body what types of activities the host country will consider authorizing and how such activity types would contribute to mitigation in the host country and in achievement of its nationally determined contribution.

Source: UNFCCC. 2019. Matters relating to Article 6 of the Paris Agreement: Rules, modalities, and procedures for the mechanism established by Article 6, para. 4, of the Paris Agreement. *Proposal by the President*. Bonn. https://unfccc.int/documents/204686.

---

50   A. Michaelowa et al. 2021. *Promoting Article 6 readiness in NDCs and NDC implementation plans*. Freiburg: Perspectives Climate Group GmbH. https://www.perspectives.cc/public/fileadmin/Publications/PCG-CF_Article_6_in_NDCs.pdf.

Host-Country Readiness for Article 6

Governments must carry out certain responsibilities to remain eligible to participate in Article 6 cooperation. The Paris Agreement is built on transparency and reporting rather than strong compliance mechanisms. Nevertheless, Article 6 outlines participation responsibilities that countries should meet to be able to transfer mitigation outcomes internationally. Under the Kyoto Protocol, countries that wished to take part in international emissions trading had to be "eligible for trade." The eligibility requirements included the establishment of a greenhouse gas (GHG) budget, a national system for estimating GHG emissions, and a national registry.[51] The Paris Agreement does not have the same structure and its compliance regime and does not require countries to be approved ex ante as eligible to trade. However, as part of the transparency principles of the Paris Agreement, all participating Parties must show, through ex post reporting, that they can manage their participation responsibilities.[52] The draft Article 6.2 text[53] states that each participating Party shall ensure that

(i)   it is a Party to the Paris Agreement;

(ii)   it has prepared, communicated, and is maintaining an NDC in accordance with Article 4, paragraph 2 of the Paris Agreement and decision 4/CMA.1;

(iii) it has arrangements in place for authorizing the use of internationally transferred mitigation outcomes (ITMOs) toward NDCs pursuant to Article 6, paragraph 3 of the Paris Agreement (section 4.2);[54]

(iv)   it has arrangements in place, consistent with this guidance and relevant decisions of the CMA, for tracking ITMOs; and that

(v)   it has provided the most recent national inventory report required in accordance with decision 18/CMA.1.

As discussed, both international rules and host country authorization are required for a CDM activity to transition to a mechanism under Article 6. Readiness for granting or denying authorization requires that host countries have the capacity to (i) evaluate the potential impact of transitioning CDM activities on their ability to comply with their NDC commitments, (ii) establish authorization criteria, and (iii) implement authorization procedures. CDM activities being considered for transitioning to an Article 6.2 collaboration will also require readiness on the part of the host country to perform corresponding adjustments.[55]

If there is an end date for authorizing transition, the host country may face pressure to have the authorization process operational as quickly as possible. A short time frame could generate a "rush into the mechanism" similar to the 2012 rush into the CDM prior to the European Union (EU) deadline for accepting activities from non-LDCs. In such a situation, host countries with institutional capacity limitations would be disadvantaged (footnote 14).

An added pressure on host countries would arise if activities were proposed to undergo a two-stage authorization caused by their delaying de-registration under the CDM until it is fully clear whether their application for Article 6.4 authorization will be granted or not. This would require a conditional authorization followed by a confirmation of CDM de-registration before final authorization is granted. Such complications require that host country transition authorization criteria and processes are clear and transparent for owners of CDM activities.

---

[51]   UNFCCC. 2001. *The Marrakesh Accords and The Marrakesh Declaration.* https://unfccc.int/cop7/documents/accords_draft.pdf.

[52]   A. Michaelowa et al. 2020. *Promoting transparency in Article 6.* Freiburg: Perspectives Climate Group GmbH. https://www.perspectives.cc/public/fileadmin/Publications/PCG_Article_6_transparency_Nov2020.pdf.

[53]   UNFCCC. 2019. Draft Text on Matters relating to Article 6 of the Paris Agreement: Guidance on cooperative approaches referred to in Article 6, para. 2, of the Paris Agreement. Version 3. 15 December. https://unfccc.int/sites/default/files/resource/DT.CMA2_.i11a.v3_0.pdf.

[54]   Arrangements in place consistent with the guidance includes the ability to perform corresponding adjustments.

[55]   This readiness requirement may also apply to activities transitioning to the Article 6.4 mechanism, depending on the results of the negotiations.

Approaches to Clean Development Mechanism Transition Assessment

Authorization will take place under Article 6.2 as well as Article 6.4 (A6.4). In the former case, the format of the authorization will likely not be guided or governed by UNFCCC rules. Under Article 6.4, the authorization is expected to be submitted to the Supervisory Body (SB) in advance of the registration of a mitigation action as a A6.4 mechanism activity and may, therefore, contain specific information as required by the SB in a designated format.

What form host country authorization criteria will take is unknown. Host countries may decide to provide blanket authorizations for private and public entities to participate in Article 6.4 Mechanism activities. At the other extreme, they may perform authorizations on a case-by-case basis. An Organisation for Economic Co-operation and Development (OECD)-report discusses these options in detail (footnote 43). A blanket authorization or assessment would require a minimum level of host country administrative capacity since no consideration of the diversity of the CDM portfolio would need to be considered. Blanket authorizations would also require the least effort by owners of CDM activities.

Authorization criteria adopted for specific groups of activities, for example, by sector, activity type, activity scale, crediting period, latest issuance, and others) would require more administrative capacity than a blanket assessment. The potential usefulness to a host country of such criteria depends on the diversity of CDM activities registered in the country. Preparatory work by the government would include a technical assessment on how to best group the activities, and development of assessment criteria for each of the groups and the translation of assessment results into nationally appropriate criteria.

Finally, a host country can perform case-by-case assessments and authorizations. Among ADB's developing member countries (DMCs) 23 out of 40 host 10 activities or less, for these countries this may not be cumbersome. For countries that host many CDM activities that are eligible internationally for transition, this is likely to require significant resources. A case-by-case assessment would also be more time-consuming as it likely would involve multiple exchanges with the owners of activities, assessing documentation that can substantiate eligibility based on national criteria in addition to confirmation of CDM de-registration. The advantage would be that the host country would be to assess the impact on the NDC emissions balance from each activity. Doing so could, however, raise equity issues depending on the criteria applied.

Implications for Developing Member Countries as Host Countries

For all DMCs, it is important to consider the implications, if any, of the agreements made in the negotiations regarding the transition of CDM activities and certified emission reductions (CERs) on their potential to participate in the mechanisms emerging under Article 6. These considerations should inform their participation in the negotiations.

For DMCs with registered CDM activities, it is important to consider how re-registration of CDM activities that they host to Article 6 mechanisms may impact the achievement of their NDC targets, especially if corresponding adjustments have to be applied. This must be considered regardless of a case-by-case, group, or blanket assessment approach to authorizing transitions is applied. A blanket assessment may lead to non-additional activities being authorized, which may jeopardize achievement of the NDC.

For DMCs that host registered CDM activities, it would be useful to assess the process of CDM transition in terms of the capacities of their institutions that will shoulder operational responsibilities. The host country needs to make important decisions and implement procedures for authorizing the re-registration of activities. First, the host country can consider what approach it will adopt to assessing and authorizing activities for re-registration under Article 6.4:

(i)   An assessment on a case-by-case basis, involving exchanges with owners, would require resources and capacity. This should be possible in countries with limited portfolios, but it could be a real challenge in countries with large portfolios.

(ii) Are there activity types that the host country government do not prefer to transition or should promote to transition? For instance, the host country may be keen to support vulnerable activities, or activities within a sector that is subject to limited policy and measures for mitigation. This would require an upfront analysis of the host country, determining what "batches" or groups of activities should be eligible for transition.

(iii) A blanket assessment and default authorization of all activities would not be demanding, but for countries with many CDM activities, could involve risk of jeopardizing the achievement of NDC targets since it would lead to significant uncertainties, e.g., in assessing the aggregated potential impact of individual activities on the NDC emission balance of the host Party.

CDM host countries would also gain from estimating what they can expect in terms of transition volumes. How many CDM activities are likely to ask for transition? If many activities are expected to transition, this would require an administrative effort from the host country. This would, however, also depend on what options are available to the owners of activities. Some CDM activities may be de-registered from the CDM and transition to the voluntary or domestic carbon crediting markets.

Finally, what kind of institutional capacity is required in the short term? Participation in Article 6 will require a designated national authority to have more capacity and assume new responsibilities that range from NDC accounting to setting up the necessary institutional infrastructure to authorize Article 6.4 projects. Until such a body is established and fully operational, interim institutional solutions may be required.

Irrespective of the outcomes on the transition of CDM activities and CERs in the 26th Conference of Parties (COP26) in Glasgow, host countries with experience in the CDM need to ensure that the human resources including experience, knowledge, as well as institutional capacity created under the CDM should not go to waste. These experiences and expertise, not only in the governance level, but also in the methodological as well as project level, are relevant to operationalizing international carbon markets as envisaged under Article 6 of the Paris Agreement.

7. Conclusion

This study has covered the transition of three different parts of the Clean Development Mechanism (CDM): (i) baseline and monitoring methodologies and relevant components of the international institutional infrastructure; (ii) activities (i.e., CDM projects and Programs of Activities [POAs]); and (iii) emissions credits such as Certified Emission Reductions (CERs).

This study highlights that transitioning the relevant CDM infrastructure to Article 6 is not controversial as it is mainly a question of agreeing on a process at the international level. Transition of methodologies is somewhat contested, but there are indications that CDM methodologies may be transitioned if complemented by tools that enable consistency with Article 6 principles. Similarly, there seems to be general agreement that at least some activities that meet Article 6.4 eligibility criteria and are re-authorized by their host countries should be allowed to transition into the Paris Agreement under Article 6.4. However, two issues that have yet to be resolved are what those eligibility criteria will be (which will be determined by Parties through negotiation) and how transitions will be implemented, i.e., the transition rules and associated transition costs, which also will involve priorities and criteria determined by host countries.

It may be possible to agree to registration cutoff dates as eligibility criteria for the transition of both CDM activities and credits. For the host countries in Asia and the Pacific, applying a cutoff date as a criterion for the transition of activities would have a strong impact on the volume of activities that can be transitioned. Currently, in ADB's developing member countries (DMCs), only about a third of the registered projects remain active. A late registration cutoff date would mean that DMC host countries with large portfolios (the People's Republic of China, Malaysia, Thailand, and Viet Nam) would have no or close to no activities eligible for transition. A late cutoff date seems to favor least developed countries (LDCs) in Asia and the Pacific.

However, the third and final iteration of the Madrid text indicates that the criteria for transitioning CDM activities may not include a cutoff date but, rather, only a deadline for completing the transition process (which includes CDM de-registration re-registration under the new Article 6.4 mechanism or a 6.2 mechanism). This would be contingent on the ability to quickly set up the Article 6.4 infrastructure and could lead to a stampede of activity developers like the one witnessed under the CDM in 2012 that could overwhelm regulators. Creation of a fast track for small- and micro-scale activities and POAs, which is not contested, would benefit the LDCs.

The transition of CERs is highly controversial and one of the challenges is how to estimate the volume that is available for transition and CERs that still could be issued. Estimating "dormant" CERs is very difficult; estimates in the literature diverge widely depending on key assumptions regarding the continued operation of activities, continued monitoring, and the degree to which crediting periods have been renewed. Issuances have not been requested for a large share of emissions reductions achieved between 2013 and 2020, but no robust estimates can be made. Published estimates vary between 2 billion to 4 billion "dormant" CERs.

Regarding already issued CERs, a total of over 700 million (42%) of the Asia and Pacific region have not yet been used, compared to a global average of 55%. This relatively good performance is dominated by the PRC and India that have been able to sell over 60% of the issued CERs; for 14 out of 25 countries from the region, over 70% of CERs remain unused. For POAs, almost 90% of CERs remain unused. With regards to their transition, the choice of cutoff date has a large impact also for CER transition in the region. In total, about 430 million unused CERs can transition under a 2008 registration cutoff date from Asia and the Pacific. However, this volume falls to 75 million for the 2013 and just 4 million for the 2016 cutoff. For later cutoff dates, activity types shift from hydro and wind to energy efficiency and solar.

For all ADB DMC countries, the agreements made in the negotiations regarding the transition of CDM activities and CERs can influence their potential to participate in international carbon markets under Article 6. These considerations should inform their participation in the negotiations. In addition, there is a need to plan and think of institutional requirements and necessary steps needed once international rules are agreed upon. For instance, the host countries can already start considering what approach it will adopt to assessing and authorizing activities for registration under Article 6.4 and utilizing that also for activities transitioning from the CDM.

Finally, the resources accrued through investment in the CDM in both the public and private sectors—including experience, knowledge, and institutional capacity—are broadly acknowledged as valuable and applicable to international carbon markets under the Paris Agreement, and the experience and expertise acquired—with respect to governance, methodological approaches, and project administration and operation—are still relevant. Irrespective of the outcome of negotiations on issues related to CDM transition, it is of utmost importance to ensure that the human, institutional, and technical capacity gained with engagement with the CDM is transferred to develop international carbon markets as envisaged under the Paris Agreement.

In the lead-up to 26th Conference of Parties (COP26) in Glasgow, there is anticipation for the finalization of the Article 6 Rulebook and advancing toward operationalizing Article 6 of the Paris Agreement. CDM transition will, no doubt, be an important issue to enable this result. Discussions at Subsidiary Body for Scientific and Technological Advice (SBSTA) in June show that the key issues remain on the table and that key lines of divergence still exist. Informal technical dialogues prior to COP26 cover issues related to what decisions are needed, how the issues relate to the overall Article 6 negotiation package and Glasgow outcome, as well as what conditions for transition should be. Agreement on elements of CDM transition will be important, if not required, for landing the whole Article 6 package.

Appendix: Certified Emission Reductions Transition Options—Subsidiary Body for Scientific and Technological Advice Chair's Summary, June 2021

Option	Sub-Option	Sub-Option II	Arguments
No use of any Kyoto units toward NDCs			No carry-over from the Kyoto Protocol to the Paris Agreement is allowed; the new 6.4 mechanism should not be overloaded by old units; it would undermine overall mitigation in global emissions in the 6.4 mechanism; creating a big hole in ambition only for the benefit of a small group of Parties that wish to use CERs, so it is not equitable to allow it.
CERs may be used toward NDCs	A CDM host Party can use CERs from its own country		It is up to each Party how it meets its NDC.
	Any Party may use CERs		The CERs represent real, additional, and verified emission reductions that have been achieved
The CERs meet certain conditions	The CDM activity from which the CERs are achieved has a registration date on or after X date	No date limitations for CDM activity registration are required	This limitation would be unfair to Host Parties that have only a few CDM activities that are registered as compared to the Host Parties that have many registered CDM activities.
		Dates per the second draft Presidency Text (2013/X/2016)	
	The CERs were issued in respect of emission reductions or removals achieved by X date	No date restriction applies	A date restriction is arbitrary as there is no difference between CERs produced in different years; other technical solutions that could be used to avoid flooding the market and those could be considered.
		Date restriction operationalised based on monitoring periods	Monitoring may be more relevant than registration date
	The CERs are used toward the NDC by X date:	31 December 2030	Use could be by the end of the first NDC cycle to enable the Party to manage that use.
		Further work is needed to assess by when such CERs would be required to be used.	The deadline in the draft Presidency texts would require further work. Use-by dates would need to be later, due to the delay since Madrid
		No use-date is needed where the CERs are from the Host Party that is using the CERs.	Any deadline would be arbitrary.

continued on next page

Appendix table *continued*

Option	Sub-Option	Sub-Option II	Arguments
A total maximum volume of CERs that may be used is set by the CMA	A maximum use cap for any non-host Party using CERs		
	A maximum volume from each CDM activity		
Use of CERs would be implemented through methods specified by the CMA	The CERs are moved to the 6.4 registry and retagged for use for NDCs		Requiring the CERs to have been retagged to enable reporting and accounting per the 6.2 guidance; moving CERs for NDC use by the Host Party enables the Host Party to be able to use them.
	The CERs are placed in a reserve for use toward NDCs		This could be good for the 6.4 mechanism as it could be used to protect against price fluctuations.
	No further requirements		The reporting requirements are sufficient to identify the CERs.
Reporting in relation to CERs used toward NDCs is in accordance with the enhanced transparency framework			CERs used toward NDCs by the Host Party and the using Party would be required to be reported in accordance with the enhanced transparency framework and the reporting requirements of the 6.2 guidance.
	The units would be required to be identified as pre-2021 CERs		This is necessary for reporting and accounting for ITMOs per the 6.2 guidance.
	Identification as pre-2021 CERs is not necessary.		
Accounting requirements in relation to CERs used toward NDCs	The Host Party is not required to apply a corresponding adjustment per 6.2 guidance, non-Host Parties do apply a corresponding adjustment		Non-Host Parties apply a corresponding adjustment because the CER has been internationally transferred.
	Any Party using pre-2021 CERs toward its NDC is required to apply a corresponding adjustment per 6.2 guidance		The host Party is required to apply a corresponding adjustment because the CER is from the time period before the start of the NDC. Non-Host Parties apply a 6 corresponding adjustment because the CER has been internationally transferred and the CER is from the time period before the start of the NDC.

CDM = Clean Development Mechanism, CER = Certified Emission Reduction, CMA = Conference of the Parties serving as the meeting of the Parties to the Paris Agreement, ITMO = internationally transferred mitigation outcome, NDC = nationally determined contribution, SBSTA = Subsidiary Body for Scientific and Technological Advice.

Sources: Authors' elaboration of Chair's summary; informal consultations and informal technical expert dialogue on Article 6 of the Paris Agreement Clean Development Mechanism activity transition to the Article 6.4 mechanism; 2021 sessions of the subsidiary bodies (May–June) SBSTA draft agenda item 15 Matters related to Article 6 of the Paris Agreement. https://unfccc.int/sites/default/files/resource/IN.SBSTA2021.i15b.pdf.

References

Asian Development Bank (ADB). 2020. *Carbon Offsetting International Aviation: Challenges and Opportunities.* Manila. http://dx.doi.org/10.22617/TCS200369-2.

ADB. 2020. *Decoding Article 6 of the Paris Agreement. Version II.* Manila. https://www.adb.org/publications/decoding-article-6-paris-agreement-v2.

ADB. 2019. *Article 6 of the Paris Agreement: Drawing Lessons from the Joint Crediting Mechanism.* Manila. https://doi.org/10.22617/TIM190555-2.

B. Amarjargal et al. 2020. *Achieving Nationally Determined Contributions through Market Mechanisms in Asia and the Pacific.* Manila. Asian Development Bank. https://doi.org/10.22617/WPS200088-2.

D. Brescia et al. 2019. *Transition Pathways for the Clean Development Mechanism under Article 6 of the Paris Agreement. Options and Implications for International Negotiators.* Freiburg: Perspectives Climate Group. https://ercst.org/wp-content/uploads/2021/01/Transition_pathways_for_the_CDM_2019-1.pdf.

M. Cames et al. 2016. *How Additional is the Clean Development Mechanism? Analysis of Application of Current Tools and Proposed Alternatives.* Berlin: Öko-Institut e.V. CLIMA.B.3/SERI2013/0026r. https://www.atmosfair.de/wp-content/uploads/clean_dev_mechanism_en.pdf.

Climate Analytics. 2019. *Article 6 Needs Ambition, Not Time Wasting.* Berlin. https://climateanalytics.org/media/carry_over_ca_briefing_11dec2019.pdf.

T. Day et al. 2019. *Supporting Vulnerable CDM Projects through Credit Purchase Facilities. Discussion Paper.* Berlin: German Emissions Trading Authority (DEHSt). https://newclimate.org/wp-content/uploads/2020/01/discussion-paper_supporting_vulnerable_CDM.pdf.

H. Fearnehough et al. 2018. *Offset Credit Supply Potential for CORSIA.* Climate Change 37/2020. Umweltbundesamt, Dessau-Roßlau.https://www.umweltbundesamt.de/en/publikationen/offset-credit-supply-potential-for-corsia.

T. Forth and F. Wolke. 2020. The Transition Question, Identifying Realistic Numbers for Negotiations on Article 6. *Carbon Mechanisms Review.* Issue No. 2. Wuppertal Institute for Climate, Environment and Energy. https://www.carbon-mechanisms.de/fileadmin/media/dokumente/Publikationen/CMR/CMR_02_2020_The_Transition_Controversy.pdf.

J. Fuessler et al. 2019. *Article 6 in the Paris Agreement as an Ambition Mechanism: Options and Recommendations.* Final Report. Zurich: Swedish Energy Agency. https://www.carbonlimits.no/wp-content/uploads/2019/07/Ambition-Raising-and-Article-6-Final.pdf.

J. Fuessler, S. La Hoz Theuer, and L. Schneider. 2019. *Transitioning Elements of the Clean Development Mechanism to the Paris Agreement.* Discussion Paper. Berlin: German Emissions Trading Authority (DEHSt). https://www.dehst.de/SharedDocs/downloads/EN/project-mechanisms/discussion-papers/transitioning_elements.pdf?__blob=publicationFile&v=2.

S. Greiner et al. 2017. *CDM Transition to Article 6 of the Paris Agreement. Options Report.* Climate Focus. https://www.climatefocus.com/sites/default/files/CDM%20Transition%20Options%20Report%20v2.0.pdf.

S. Greiner et al. 2020. *Article 6 Piloting: State of Play and Stakeholder Experiences.* Climate Focus (CF) and Perspectives Climate Group (PCG). https://www.perspectives.cc/public/fileadmin/user_upload/PCG_CF_Article_6_Piloting_Dec_2020.pdf.

S. Hoch et al. 2020. Closing the Deal on 'CDM Transition' – How COP 25 Defined New Guardrails for Compromise and What they Mean for Africa. Climate Finance Innovators. https://www.climatefinanceinnovators.com/wp-content/uploads/2020/05/Closing-the-deal-on-CDM-Transition_web.pdf.

Institute for Global Environmental Strategies (IGES). 2021. *Nationally Determined Contributions (NDC) Database, version 7.4.* (accessed 15 August 2021). https://pub.iges.or.jp/pub/iges-ndc-database.

T. Ishikawa et al. 2020. *CDM supply potential for emission reductions up to the end of 2020.* Institute for Global Environmental Strategies, Mitsubishi UFJ Research and Consulting Co., Ltd., NewClimate – Institute for Climate Policy and Global Sustainability gGmbH and Öko-Institut. https://www.oeko.de/fileadmin/oekodoc/CDM-supply-potential-for-emission-reductions-up-to-the-end-of-2020.pdf.

N. Kraemer, S. Greiner, and M. v. Unger. 2019. *The CDM Legal Context Post-2020.*Climate Focus / Atlas Environmental Law Advisory. 21 August https://www.climatefocus.com/sites/default/files/ClimateFocus_Atlas_2019_CDM_Post_2020.pdf.

A.Y. Lo and R. Cong. 2017. After CDM: Domestic Carbon Offsetting in China. *Journal of Cleaner Production.* Vol. 141. pp. 1391–1399.

L. Lo Re and J. Ellis. 2021. Operationalising the Article 6.4 mechanism: Options and implications of CDM activity transition and new activity registration. *Climate Change Expert Group Paper* No. 2021/02. Paris: IEA and OECD., OECD Publishing, Paris. https://doi.org/10.1787/08ce04ee-en.

L. Lo Re and M. Vaidyula. 2019. Markets Negotiations under the Paris Agreement a technical analysis of two unresolved issues. *Climate Change Expert Group Paper* No. 2019(3). Paris: International Energy Agency (IEA) and Organisation for Economic Co-operation and Development (OECD). https://www.oecd.org/env/cc/Markets-negotiations-under-the-Paris-Agreement-a-technical-analysis-of-two-unresolved-issues.pdf.

A. Marcu. 2017. Governance of Article 6 of the Paris Agreement and Lessons Learned from the Kyoto Protocol. *Fixing Climate Governance Series Paper* No. 4. Centre for International Governance Innovation. https://www.cigionline.org/static/documents/documents/Fixing%20Climate%20Governance%20Paper%20no.4%20WEB.pdf.

A. Marcu and V. K. Duggal. 2019. *Negotiations on Article 6 of the Paris Agreement–Road to Madrid. Manila: Asian Development Bank.* http://dx.doi.org/10.22617/WPS190559-2.

A. Marcu, S. Kanda, and D. Agrotti. 2021. *CDM Transition: CER Availability.* Bruxelles: European Roundtable on Climate Change and Sustainable Transition (ERCST). https://ercst.org/wp-content/uploads/2021/01/20201020-CDM-transition-paper.pdf.

A. Michaelowa. 2005. *Creating the foundations for host country participation in the CDM: experiences and challenges in CDM capacity building,* in F. Yamin, ed. *Climate change and carbon markets. A handbook of emission reduction mechanisms.* London: Earthscan. pp. 305–320.

A. Michaelowa et al. 2019. Additionality Revisited: Guarding the Integrity of Market Mechanisms under the Paris Agreement. *Climate Policy.* Vol. 19(10). pp. 1211–1224. https://doi.org/10.1080/14693062.2019.1628695.

A. Michaelowa et al. 2020. *CDM method transformation: updating and transforming CDM methods for use in an Article 6 context.* Perspectives and Climate Focus. Freiburg. https://www.perspectives.cc/public/fileadmin/Publications/CDM_method_transf_report_accessible.pdf.

A. Michaelowa et al. 2020. *Promoting transparency in Article 6.* Perspectives. Freiburg. https://www.perspectives.cc/public/fileadmin/Publications/PCG_Article_6_transparency_Nov2020.pdf.

A. Michaelowa et al. 2021. *Promoting Article 6 readiness in NDCs and NDC implementation plans.* Perspectives. Freiburg. https://www.perspectives.cc/public/fileadmin/Publications/PCG-CF_Article_6_in_NDCs.pdf.

A. Michaelowa et al. 2021. *Volumes and types of unused Certified Emission Reductions (CERs).* Perspectives and ZHAW. Freiburg and Zurich. https://www.perspectives.cc/public/fileadmin/Publications/PCG-ZHAW_unused_CERs_PAC.pdf.

A. Michaelowa, H-M. Ahonen, and A. Espelage. 2021. *Setting crediting baselines under Article 6 of the Paris Agreement, CMM Working Group Discussion Paper.* Perspectives, Freiburg. https://www.perspectives.cc/public/fileadmin/user_upload/CMM-WG_Art_6_baselines_Final_layouted_v2__002_.pdf.

A. Michaelowa, A. Espelage, and B. Müller. 2020. *Negotiating Cooperation under Article 6 of the Paris Agreement. European Capacity Building Initiative.* https://www.perspectives.cc/public/fileadmin/user_upload/Article_6_2020_PCG.pdf.

A. Michaelowa, I. Shishlov, and D. Brescia. 2019. *Evolution of international carbon markets: lessons for the Paris Agreement.* WIREs Climate Change. https://wires.onlinelibrary.wiley.com/doi/10.1002/wcc.613.

W. Obergassel and F. Asche. 2017. Shaping the Paris Mechanisms Part III: An Update on Submissions on Article 6 of the Paris Agreement," *JIKO Policy Paper* No. 05/2017. Wuppertal: Wuppertal Institute for Climate, Environment and Energy. https://www.carbon-mechanisms.de/fileadmin/media/dokumente/Publikationen/Policy_Paper/PP_2017_05_Art_6_Submissions_III_bf.pdf.

W. Obergassel and F. Asche. 2017. Shaping the Paris Mechanisms Part III: An Update on Submissions on Article 6 of the Paris Agreement," *JIKO Policy Paper.* No. 01/2017. Wuppertal: Wuppertal Institute for Climate, Environment and Energy. https://epub.wupperinst.org/frontdoor/deliver/index/docId/6682/file/6682_Paris_Mechanisms.pdf.

M. Unger. 2019. *Host Country Authorizations under Article 6 Paris Agreement: Developments After COP 24 (Katowice).* Atlas Environmental Law Advisory. https://www.carbon-mechanisms.de/fileadmin/media/dokumente/Publikationen/Studie/Studie_2019_ATLAS_Host_Country_Authorizations_Art_6_eng.pdf.

United Nations Development Programme (UNDP). 2006. *The Clean Development Mechanism – An Assessment of Progress.* New York. https://www.uncclearn.org/sites/default/files/inventory/undp34.pdf.

UNEP DTU Partnership. 2021. UNEP DTU CDM/JI Pipeline Analysis and Database. https://www.cdmpipeline.org/ (accessed 7 September 2021).

United Nations Framework Convention on Climate Change (UNFCCC). 2015. Adoption of the Paris Agreement. *Decision* 1/CP.21. Bonn. https://unfccc.int/resource/docs/2015/cop21/eng/10a01.pdf.

UNFCCC. 2016. *Aggregate Effect of the Intended Nationally Determined Contributions: An Update.* Synthesis Report by the Secretariat. https://unfccc.int/resource/docs/2016/cop22/eng/02.pdf.

C. Warnecke et al. 2017. *Vulnerability of CDM Projects for Discontinuation of Mitigation Activities. Assessment of Project Vulnerability and Options to Support Continued Mitigation.* German Emissions Trading Authority (DEHSt). Berlin. https://newclimate.org/wp-content/uploads/2017/05/vulnerability-of-cdm.pdf.